HISPANIC, FEMALE AND YOUNG:
AN ANTHOLOGY

EDITED BY PHYLLIS TASHLIK

PIÑATA

BOOKS

Piñata Books
Houston, TX
1994

This volume is made possible through support from the National Endowment for the Arts, a federal agency, the Andrew W. Mellon Foundation and the Lila Wallace-Reader's Digest Fund.

Piñata Books
A Division of
Arte Público Press
University of Houston
Houston, Texas 77204-2090

Piñata Books are full of surprises!

Cover design and illustration by Gladys Ramírez.

Library of Congress Cataloging-in-Publication Data

Hispanic, female and young: an anthology / edited by Phyllis Tashlik.
p.
ISBN 1-55885-/080-5
1. American literature--Hispanic American authors. 2. Hispanic American women--Literary collections. 3. Hispanic American youth--Literary collections. 4. American literature--20th century.
I. Tashlik, Phyllis
PS508.H57H56 1993
810.8'09287--dc20   93-4104
                                                         CIP

The paper used in this publication meets the requirements of the American National Standard for Permanence of Paper for Printed Library Materials Z39.48-1984 ⊗

*For "Las Mujeres"
of Manhattan East*

HISPANIC, FEMALE AND YOUNG:

AN ANTHOLOGY

Table of Contents

Chapter 1: Remembering Our Culture

Chapter 2: Lo Mágico y La Realidad

Chapter 3: La Familia

Chapter 4: Recuerdo: Memories from Childhood

Chapter 5: Growing Up

Chapter 6: A Las Mujeres

Chapter 7: El Barrio

Chapter 8: Prejudice

Chapter 9: Making It

Introduction

We began in a circle. Twelve eighth-grade girls met with me, their teacher, on a sunny September afternoon, in an ancient red brick public schoolhouse on East 99th Street in Spanish Harlem ("El Barrio"). We were pioneering an elective named "Las Mujeres Hispanas," a class designed to introduce Hispanic teenage girls to Hispanic female literature and to their own potential as writers.

Slowly, tentatively, they began to share their life stories. Sara spoke of being "half-Mexican" and Monique of being "half-Cuban." Others offered tales of family journeys to the United States from Puerto Rico, Colombia, Panama. Our group represented a mosaic of cultures, histories, and backgrounds. I recall the words of Olga Méndez, the state senator the girls would later interview. She cautioned them that all people should know and be proud of their roots, that simply being called Hispanic isn't sufficient when your background is Puerto Rican, Dominican, or Mexican.

For my young "mujeres," this classroom experience was definitely strange. It was probably the first time they had been asked to share in school their perception of themselves as young women and Latinas. There we were, a huddled group of females discussing our lives, while eighth-grade boys gathered outside the closed classroom door. We could see their heads bobbing up and down as they sought the girls' attention and organized a mild protest against an all-girls' class in our small, alternative school. The class may not have seemed right to the boys, but the girls saw it as an honor and a personal mission. As they later wrote in the introduction to the first anthology of their written work:

> A class like Las Mujeres is something that
> helps you learn about yourself and others and

find compassion in your heart to appreciate other cultures while finding in yourself who you really are. Las Mujeres helped us to understand ourselves in a better way. To take charge of our lives. To look at the world in a better way.

We feel proud of contributing to such a project. We have been learning about what makes us special as Hispanics and what we value in life as women. We have learned from all our experiences...so that now we have an idea about the future, what it could hold, and how we can make it better not only for ourselves but for others too.

This was a class I had wanted to see happen for a long time. When the possibility presented itself through the Apple Corporation's Educational Grants Project, I reached for it, writing a two-year proposal and obtaining for our school several Macintosh computers, a laser printer, and funds to purchase books. With additional support from the Manhattan East directors (Lynn Kearney and Adele Gittleman), staff (especially Betty Carra, Jesus Fraga, Marsha Lipsitz, and Kenny Solomon) and Community School District 4, the East Harlem district often cited as a model for alternative school education, we launched Las Mujeres Hispanas in 1987. Libraries throughout East Harlem later displayed the students' writing and other NYC schools, such as Urban Academy, sponsored similar classes.

The need for Las Mujeres became obvious to me when designing the literature curriculum for our racially and economically diverse group of students. My students had gone through nine years of education and, although the NYC public school population is more than a third Hispanic, they had never been introduced to a single novel written by a Hispanic author and certainly not by a female Hispanic author. They had been denied the richness of their own literary tradition and the inspiration of Hispanic women whose lives challenged North American stereotypes.

Once our meetings as a group were well established, the girls began their first research project: a survey of textbooks approved by the board of education. They discovered that most of the available books included few Hispanic writers and that of them only three were women. The final tally was disappointing and Millie Rivera, the student who analyzed the survey's results, wrote:

> We knew that good literature, stories that really appealed to us, was available, but publishers were excluding them from their books.
>
> Our main purpose has been to make the Hispanic woman noticeable, not only to other girls our age, but to many people. So, it's going to take a long time and hard work to get literature by Hispanics into students' textbooks.

Our goals were clear. The girls worked hard and, like all writers, spent long hours writing, editing and reading. They became computer literate and at times felt they were simply confiding their thoughts and feelings to the familiar computer monitor. Their writing, however, went beyond private confidences. They shared everything they wrote, often writing as partnerships or groups. When they interviewed Hispanic women whom they admired, each girl wrote her own version of the interview and we then used the computer to weave together sections of their work into one cohesive piece. In that way we captured the words of Nicholas Mohr, author; Tina Ramírez, dancer and founder of Ballet Hispánico; Ingrid Ramos, a beloved teacher; and Olga Méndez, New York State senator (Chapter 9: "Making It").

In addition to writing, an integral part of our project was reading literature by female Hispanic authors. We had an auspicious beginning since we chose *Nilda* by Nicholasa Mohr. The story's setting was our own East Harlem, and the streets Nicholasa wrote about were the streets the girls walked each day on their way to school. The division between fiction and reality blurred considerably, especially when Nicholasa visited our group and the students learned of the similarity between her life and the character's life. The girls loved *Nilda* and they loved Nicholasa, and that was the beginning of our foray into fiction by Latinas. Favorite books were later circulated among classmates, friends outside the school, and, especially, mothers. We became a community of readers.

The girls devoured each set of books that arrived, searching for novels, stories, and poems that appealed to them and that they thought would appeal to other young teenagers. We also frequented El Centro de Estudios Puertorriqueños at Hunter College to read back issues of such journals as *Revista Chicano-Riqueña* and *The Americas Review*, hoping to discover the voices of other female Hispanic writers. Our priorities were the opposite of most literature classes; instead of the students being assigned an "approved" pre-selected body of literature to be read and analyzed, they selected the literature to be read and made judgments about its appeal to the young adult reader. Most of the selections in this book were the result of that collaborative effort.

The chapters that follow represent what was most meaningful to the girls committed to the goals of "Las Mujeres." Their areas of interest—culture, magic, the family and community, growing up, prejudice—emerged from our discussions, writing, experiences, and reading. In the chapter "Remembering Our Culture," for example, they sometimes treasure their heritage, like Sara Rodríguez who retells the legend of La Llorona, the ghost who floats through the woods, crying out for her children ("Half-Mexican"). Sometimes they drift from their heritage, as María Persons describes in "Losing Your Culture": "I don't care enough to spend two years of my life searching for my identity." Nevertheless, they all responded to Lorna Dee Cervantes' poem "Refugee Ship" and its image of "a ship that never docks / a ship that never docks."

Most of their own writing, especially in the chapters on

family and community, is concerned with the reality of their daily lives. Leslie Rivera entitles her piece "A Day in the Life of Me, Leslie" and begins, "It's me in real life. And what an awful life I lead," a life filled with the challenge of being an adolescent. They write of other girls whose lives are cut short, of a friend who is still young but "fighting as if she were in a jungle, as if a lion, were chasing her, as if her life were catching her before her time" ("Caught by Life" by Edna Robles). Many depict the life of their community, sometimes to praise it and sometimes to express their fears. When they try fiction, they root it in a familiar urban landscape of crowded apartment buildings, bold cockroaches, bustling streets, teenagers hanging out in parks. In "Corazón," the authors' references to suburbia don't have the same ring of truth as their descriptions of city life; the sequence of events bears some resemblance to familiar *telenovelas*, the Spanish-speaking soap operas they often watched with their mothers, aunts, and sisters. In their stories, however, the girl gets to turn down the guy ("I Thought You Loved Me" by Michelle Calero).

Despite all their emphasis on realism, the girls also enjoyed literature that spoke of magic and mysticism. After all, they are the heirs of *magia* and *santería* and cowrie shells, traditions some of their grandmothers have instructed them in. They chose literature that steps into the realm of *brujas*—"Dream in the Hospital" by Rosa María Arenas and Obatala, King of Spirits in "Listening to Mongo Santamaría Calling the Spirits from Buffalo" by Olga Mendell—and of deceased relatives who inhabit a large mirror in the family dining room ("In the Family" by María Elena Llano).

The chapter on prejudice practically wrote itself. Prejudice is part of their everyday experience, to be accused of trying to be "white" or of trying to be "black," or as María writes, to be questioned about whether they "'sound' Spanish, or 'look' Spanish, or 'dress' Spanish" until they're no longer sure if they *are* Spanish. The conflicts Lorna Dee Cervantes writes about in "Which Line is This? I Forget" echo their own experiences: "Where the rules are rigid/and the stakes are high/and you play for keeps." Although many of the girls are second-generation U.S. citizens, they still have to confront the conflicts their parents faced a generation before. Perhaps these issues are more public now and less lonely; nonetheless, they are far from settled, as becomes painfully clear in Inez Santana's "Laughing Last" in the prejudiced conversations she overhears during a subway ride.

The young women who worked on this collection hope to change the status quo. We hope that when young people read these stories and poems, they will see—perhaps for the first time—their lives confirmed and their culture valued in literature.

Like "las mujeres," most of us grow up somewhere in between two cultures, one brought by us or our families and the amalgam that is U.S. culture. We are a multicultured nation, and this volume demonstrates that in addition to celebrating the ties that bind, we must also honor the cultures that distinguish us and give pride to our families and meaning to our lives.

Phyllis Tashlik
Autumn 1993

CHAPTER 1

REMEMBERING OUR CULTURE

El Olvido
(según las madres)

by Judith Ortiz Cofer

It is a dangerous thing
to forget the climate of
your birthplace; to choke out
the voices of the dead relatives when
in dreams they call you by
your secret name; dangerous
to spurn the clothes you were
born to wear for the sake of fashion;
to use weapons and sharp instruments you
are not familiar with; dangerous
to disdain the plaster saints before
which your mother kneels praying for you with
embarrassing fervor that you survive in
the place you have chosen to live; a costly,
bare and elegant room with no pictures
on the walls: a forgetting place where
she fears you might die of exposure.
Jesús, María y José.
El olvido is a dangerous thing.

GETTING TO KNOW MY MOM

by Luz Otero

We were in my house after dinner. I was washing the dishes when I remembered that I had to interview my mother, Eva Otero. My mother is a bit shorter than I am. She has short, medium brown hair. Her eyes are a joyful brown. She is very strict but cares a lot for her children. I called her, and she didn't answer. So, as usually happens, I went to her and I said, "Mom, I want to interview you for 'Las Mujeres.'" And she said, "No, I'm busy now, and after I finish this, I have to watch my favorite soap opera, that is 'Mi Amada Beatriz.'"

I said, "But Mom, I have to do this today, it's due tomorrow."

She said, "Okay, but don't keep me here waiting for you to ask a question." I ran to the kitchen and grabbed the nearest pen, then returned to the living room. When she came to the living room, I told her to sit near me so that I wouldn't have to make her repeat the answers she gave me. As she told me the answers to the questions, she told me things that I never knew about her life.

When my mother first came to New York from Puerto Rico, she was fourteen years old. She came because my grandmother told her that there were better chances of getting a job and better schools in New York. She also came because the economy in Puerto Rico was not that good, and the family couldn't afford for her to stay with them anymore. In Puerto Rico, if you got a job, the boss gave you a salary that is half of what you could get here.

When she came to New York, she found a lot of differences in the way Puerto Ricans lived and the way the Americans lived. Of course, there was the difference in the language. She never had learned how to speak English.

Now she is going to a school named SCI on 14th Street to learn English. But there were other differences. For instance, the foods. In Puerto Rico the spices and the food were more nutritious and fresh. Some foods that she missed were beans, rice, sofrito, and plátanos.

Transportation was different, too. In New York there were so many trains and special buses. In Puerto Rico there was only one bus, and the driver took you directly to where you wanted to go. She depended on her sister and her brother-in-law to take her to school and other places in New York because she didn't know her way around. That is why life for her in New York was hard.

Also, the prices were higher in New York. She was afraid that she would be poor and homeless in the street. She was really surprised when her sister told her that in New York there was public assistance and Medicaid. She was very astounded because they didn't have anything like that in Puerto Rico. She had to follow many steps to get accepted for welfare. Welfare gave her a monthly check for her clothes, food, and rent. That is how she managed to keep up with the high prices, until she got married.

Sometimes my aunt didn't make my mother feel comfortable in New York. This made my mother very lonely, and she sometimes wished that she could go back to Puerto Rico. But she was able to make other friends, and that is the most important thing.

She got married because there wasn't anybody to warn her about how important it is to have a good future, to work, and have a good career. But she's satisfied. She told me that if she wouldn't be living in New York, she would have been in the streets of Puerto Rico looking for a job with at least ten children. But in New York her mind has been kept active, and she has become more interested in school and other things instead of just in having children. For her, life in New York has been very special.

My mother went to Charles E. Hughes High School for four years and graduated when she was eighteen. In those times, Hughes was an advanced high school. She made a lot of Latin American friends from Ecuador, El Salvador, Puerto Rico, and New York. She never had to deal with racial conflicts because she got along with all of her friends.

My mother doesn't care if her children follow the Puerto Rican customs. She doesn't really care if her children dress in school uniforms like the way Puerto Rican children used to dress. She wants us to be the way we are. Also, in Puerto Rico the children had to be in early, but here my mother allows us to stay out until about eight o'clock at night.

One of the things my mother dislikes the most about New York is having drugs in the neighborhood. Sometimes she feels like moving out of her apartment and going somewhere that drugs don't exist. But she says, "That's impossible because drugs exist everywhere." Even in Puerto Rico you can find drugs, although when she went to visit her parents who live in the same house where she grew up, she didn't see any drugs. She visits Puerto Rico almost every year, and sometimes she wishes to stay and never come back.

She said that she felt comfortable answering these questions because it helped her to let out her feelings, and it cleared up things between us. I learned a lot about how my mother felt about New York, Puerto Rico, her neighborhood, and her struggles when she first came here to live. It's exciting to imagine being on your own at fourteen, but I would not want to have to try it myself.

Refugee Ship

by Lorna Dee Cervantes

Like wet cornstarch
I slide past *mi abuelita's* eyes
bible placed by her side
she removes her glasses
the pudding thickens

mamá raised me with no language
I am an orphan to my Spanish name
the words are foreign, stumbling on my tongue
I stare at my reflection in the mirror
brown skin, black hair

I feel I am a captive
aboard the refugee ship
a ship that will never dock
a ship that will never dock

Being Half-Mexican

by Sara Rodríguez

I am half-Mexican and half-Puerto Rican, but I don't really like to admit to being part Mexican. I am Puerto Rican from my father's side, and I am Mexican from my mother's side. I don't really have anything against either of them. I like the Puerto Rican customs, and I also like the Mexican customs, except for some things that I will explain.

I feel a little embarrassed about being Mexican. Why? Because when I tell my friends I am half-Mexican, they start laughing. I have a particular friend who likes to make me mad by calling me "Chicana," which means "Mexican girl." Oh, I hate that! And also because when I tell someone, they just stare at me as if I was lying.

My mother looks like a Puerto Rican, most people say so. I like that. Practically all the Mexican women have long black hair. Not my mother. Her hair is very short, and she dyes it a reddish color.

I like the way my mother cooks. It is very rare that she cooks Mexican food. Except when my uncles arrive. They are also Mexican.

My uncles come from Texas to work in New Jersey on construction jobs. They have been traveling up here for fourteen years to work for the same boss. They stay here for about a month each time. I get mad when they come because I have to give up my bed. And also because when they come my mother listens to everything they say, and then we can't do anything. For example, when one of my brothers asks my mother if he can go fishing and my uncles say something like, "No, because it's too dangerous" my mother agrees with them.

My mother is very close to my uncles, so she must cook Mexican food every day or my uncles don't eat.

My brothers and I suffer because we don't like to eat Mexican food and besides, most of the food my mother makes contains jalapeños and hot sauce. Usually, my mother will just give us money to buy food from outside, or my father cooks Puerto Rican food. Puerto Rican food is rice with beans, pork shoulder (pernil), cod fish, and fried chicken.

When my uncles leave, my mother wakes up from her Mexican dream, and she goes back to cooking Puerto Rican food.

My two sisters are Mexicans. Their father is Mexican too, but they were raised here, and they both speak English. They live in Manhattan. So on weekends they come to my house to help my mother cook. My biggest sister does the Mexican rice, and my other sister does the tacos. It all depends on what they are going to eat. (You can tell from what I choose to write about that I really do like food.)

Mexicans have a very bad way of talking. They talk with a funny accent… well, I think so. My uncles also talk very dirty. That's their way of talking. They talk to their kids like that too. When they curse, I just stare at them, like telling them, we are not in Mexico — we are in New York City. They just tell me they are used to talking that way.

This is what I feel about being Mexican, and why I feel the way I do. It isn't that bad after you get used to it. What I mean is that after people get used to knowing that I am Mexican, they treat me the same, like I am one of them.

It is nice to know you are from another place. Sometimes people like to hear Mexican jokes and stories, like one of the stories my uncle told me.

I will just tell you part of the story.

There was once a lady whose name was "La Llorna" which in English means "The Cryer." It is said that the Cryer had three kids. Anyway, they say that the Cryer was fed up with her kids, and that one day she killed them. Nights and days passed, and nothing was heard. But one day many people heard a scream, and whey they went to

25

see, the Cryer had killed herself because she regretted killing her own children.

A few days passed, and people were hearing noises at night. One night when they went out to see who it was, guess what? It was the ghost of the Cryer calling out, *"Mis hijos, mis hijos* [my kids, my kids]". Everybody ran back inside, and they heard the Cryer calling.

She used to fly to the woods and to the river to stare. In the water she would see the images of her kids. She became crazy, and she would set fire to the houses near where she used to live. The people burned her house and she was left to float around all night. People say she wandered in the woods, and they were afraid to go out at night. They never learned where in the woods she lived. And this is the end of the story. This story is always told to the kids to scare them.

I realize there are so many things I should be proud of.

Half-Cuban

by Monique Rubio

My name is Monique, and I am half-Puerto Rican and half-Cuban. It's easy being Puerto Rican because that's what most of my friends are, but it's not easy being Cuban. When I tell people I am half-Cuban, some act dumb and say "so you're a communist." That really gets me mad. Sometimes when I am in classes where the teacher is talking about Cuba, they expect me to know everything just because I am part Cuban. I know a few things about Cuba, but not little details like a specific poem a person made in Cuba during the Spanish-American War or the names of every town and city in Cuba.

One of the best parts of being Cuban is the stories my grandmother tells me about Cuba. Like how, when my dad was about ten years old, he learned to drive a jeep, and how she had an orange tree in the back of her house, and how she used to go to the bakery as a child with her brother to smell the bread and watch how they made it. These little stories make me want to go to Cuba more and more, especially when my grandmother tells me that the water is so blue and clear and the sandy beaches are so pretty. Some day I will go to Cuba, when I am an adult.

Sometimes it is even a lot of fun being Spanish because I am very fair skinned, so I look American ("white" as Spanish people sometimes say). One incident occurred when I was in a store, and the cashier was talking to her friend in Spanish and saying things like "look at that 'white girl,' she looks like such a snob, I don't like the way she looks." I understood them clearly, but I didn't say anything until I paid for my groceries. Then I said, "Thank you, have a nice day" in Spanish. The two girls looked at each other in shock and turned burning red with embarrassment. After I left the store, I could not stop laughing.

I don't know why so many people I know always refer to American people as "white" people. For example, when I first went to my school, my friends around my block thought that it was a school for white people only and they told me I would lose my Spanish roots once I went there. My two best friends from elementary school stopped talking to me, and when I did see them, they were cold and they would tell secrets to each other in front of my face. Before I was always in on the secrets.

I think this problem is more common among girls because more girls are in "clicks" than boys. Girls are more critical. With boys, if they are playing football or some other sports, they don't care who is playing: rich or poor, black or white, as long as they can play a good game. But if a few girls are playing jump rope, they might not let a certain girl play because she is poor and doesn't dress nicely or because she is rich and they are jealous.

Losing Your Culture

by María Persons

Over this winter vacation I've been thinking a lot about my family. I'm half-Spanish and half-black. My mom's family is my Spanish half. They came to this country from Colombia, South America. Her mom, my grandmother, had nine brothers and sisters (one of them died at birth), so you can understand how big my mom's family is, especially now that almost everyone has children.

There are so many people in my mom's family that I really don't consider all of my family my real family. When I think of "family," I think of having Sunday dinner together, or having someone you can call. But most of my mom's family live in Chicago, and I really don't know them very well. Maybe I'll see them once a year, and I don't feel that you can see people once a year and then consider them your family.

I feel that my family members through the generations have been losing their heritage. I'm not so much talking only about my great-uncles and great-aunts, but about their children. Many people feel that if they make a lot of money, or enough money they lose their heritage in the process. I don't feel that this is necessarily true, but in the case of some of my relatives, that might be true. Some of them don't know Spanish, and some do not want to use their Spanish names.

This writing about my relatives has made me think about my own life and how far away from my own heritage I am. I have not "decided" this to happen; it wasn't my choice at all, and I'm not very happy about it. But to tell you the truth, I don't care enough to spend two years of my life searching for my identity.

So many people have told me that I don't look Spanish or sound Spanish or dress Spanish (how can you "sound"

Spanish or "look" Spanish or "dress" Spanish?), that sometimes I really try to be "Spanish." I would tell kids I was Hispanic, but they would say, you don't look it. Why do you dress that way? You don't even speak Spanish. I know some of them didn't mean it.

But sometimes I myself am not sure if I am Spanish or not.

Interviewing my Mom, Dolores Rodríguez

by Sara Rodríguez

We sat in the dark living room. There was only a dim light from a small lamp. Sitting there, my mother watched a Spanish soap opera called "Rosa Salvaje." She was so into it that every time I asked her a question she told me to wait until a commercial came on and then she would answer it. So I just sat there studying the way I was going to ask her the question. When a commercial came on, I asked her a question and she said something like, "Oh well, when I was small I lived in . . ." Then she would stop and say she would tell me later because the *novela* (soap opera) started again. There I go again, waiting for another commercial.

When the program was finished, I finally had the chance to ask her the questions. Luckily there were no more interruptions. Before I even said a word she started to yawn. I said, "Oh no. Don't you fall asleep on me. I have to finish this interview by tomorrow."

And my mother said, "As soon as I finish the interview I will go straight to bed because I feel very tired." Then my mother took me back to a small village in Mexico called Chihuahua. That was where she was born on October 22, 1945. She lived very comfortably, and she felt free to do anything she wanted to do without anyone telling her anything.

By the age of twenty, my mother had two daughters, Martha and Elva. And she worked in a Chinese restaurant as a waitress. She left my sisters with a babysitter until she got home from work in the evening. In the restaurant she usually ate Chinese food, and she used to order some food to take home. She hardly had time to cook Mexican food, so she had to get used to eating what she ate in the restaurant. Sometimes she was asked to cook when a chef was out. The kinds of foods that she cooked were pescado al

31

vapor, chop suey, pescado a la veracruzana, and fried rice.

She wasn't sure if she should come to the U.S.A. to see how life was. She was twenty-two years old when she was thinking about making her decision. She thought that by coming over here she would find life easier, and she would make twice the money she made in Mexico. She also wanted to come here to make life easier for her daughters, such as in education and in getting to know people who were from different backgrounds.

She didn't think that the language differences would make the trip difficult because she already knew how to speak English. She had to learn because there were always tourists eating in the restaurant she worked in. In order to communicate she had to know how to speak English.

When she had me and my two brothers (in the United States), she expected us to get used to eating Mexican food because she said that one of these days we might move to Mexico. But thanks to God that time hasn't come, and we haven't gotten used to eating Mexican food. She says that she can't find the same products that she found in Mexico to use in her cooking. For example, when she bought jalapeños, a type of hot pepper, she would say something like "they aren't hot enough."

When she first went to a clinic in New York, they gave her a prescription to take to the pharmacy. When she then had to wait for half an hour or so, my mother was confused. In Mexico, medical attention was so different. They took care of you faster, and all you had to do to get the medicine you needed was to go to a drug store and ask for it. There was no waiting. When she was in Mexico, they didn't use things like nasal spray or stomach medicines. For a simple stomachache, they usually gave you tea made from some special leaves, and that was all, unless what you had was more serious.

She has travelled back and forth to Mexico about six

times. By car, it takes three days and two nights, without staying over in hotels, just resting in areas along the road in order to sleep for a few hours. It's fun traveling by car because you get to see all the animals on the farms that you pass and also all different styles of homes.

My mother feels very happy about being interviewed and about my participating in Las Mujeres Hispanas.

Lost Relatives
by Judith Ortiz Cofer

In the great diaspora
of our chromosomes,
we've lost track of one another.
Living our separate lives,
unaware of the alliance of our flesh,
we have at times recognized
our kinship through the printed word:
Classifieds, where we trade our lives
in two inch columns;
Personals, straining our bloodlines
with our lonely hearts; and
Obituaries, announcing a vacancy
in our family history
through names that call us home
with their familiar syllables.

Bedtime Story

Carolina Hospital

Before bed,
they stare attentively.
He creates the past.

He tells them of mountains,
creeks, horses and
rocking chair terraces.

They see fences,
pools, volvos and
sunken living rooms.

They beg him not to cry.

The Beauty of Me and My People

by Lorna Dee Cervantes

Funny how I never noticed it before
but there's beauty in my smooth amber skin
in the rich ginger-chocolate perfection.
It was foolish to think that pale
white, veined skin
was beauty.
My hair is also a wonder—raven black
sexy—against the whiteness of a pillow.
Thick and strong
deep and dark

                        shiny . . .
And my dark Spanish/Indian eyes
glossy and clear
a deep mahogany brown,
in dim light they blend in darkness . . .
And the dark of my eyes
And the dark of my hair
against the amber background of my skin
                paint a very pretty picture.

CHAPTER 2

LO MÁGICO Y LA REALIDAD

THey Say

by JudiTH OrTiz CofER

They say
when I arrived,
traveling light,
the women who waited
plugged
the cracks in the walls
with rags
dipped in alcohol
to keep drafts and demons out.
Candles were lit
to the Virgin.
They say
Mother's breath
kept blowing the mouth
right and left.
When I slipped
into their hands
the room was in shadows.
They say
I nearly turned away,
undoing
the hasty knot of my umbilicus.
They say
my urge to bleed
told them I was like a balloon
with a leak,
a soul trying to fly away
through the cracks in the wall.
The midwife sewed
and the women prayed
as they fitted

39

me for life
in a tight corset of gauze.
But their prayers
held me back,
the bandages held me in,
and all that night
they dipped
their bloody rags.
They say
Mother slept through it all,
blowing out
candles
with her breath.

The Poltergeist

by Carmen M. Pursifull

Too bad about Gertrude.
They say she disappeared in
view of seven witnesses.

I hear that glassware
flew in frenzied aim against
the walls   that tables
moved by unknown means and
chairs would spin in vicious
swirls   only to land quite
soundlessly upon the rug.

    Amazement at occurrence
rare   the townsfolk whispered
timidly about witches.

    Meanwhile   Gertrude
taut   strained   Gertrude
sat   eyes riveted to places
no one dared to enter.

    One day   as neighbors
peeped into her window
Gertrude turned and smiled
then slowly she was raised by
unseen hands to crash against
the skylight on the roof.
The neighbors screamed in fear
as Gertrude flew above the
splintered glass   high
higher to the sky   her broken
neck tilting an angle of
      goodbye.

41

Dream in the Hospital

by Rosa María Arenas

She said her body was broken.
She saw herself outside herself.
There were witches in a circle
weaving a spell, putting her back together
with their brooms, sweeping her up slowly
making her well and whole.

Witches putting her back together,
"Brujas con escobas," she said with musical
wonder in her voice, looking to me with that
Important Dream look.

She said witches circling, sweeping.
And even as I said "See, you're going to get better,"
I knew this was a dream of death, a dream of
impossible healing, the celestial body intact.
This was translation of fact.
But then the words,
alien and flat, were out of my mouth before I
knew I was lying.
Hearing this, her eyes
turned inward, her mouth became a
straight line. Since I
refused to understand I
disappointed her one last time.

She said witches circling.
She saw herself
outside broken.
She said witches
muttering, circling.

She saw herself broken
and they were putting her
together, las brujas.

Anita Lake Rojas

by Jeannette Tiburcio

What you are about to read is a true story. It is about a terrible incident that happened to my uncle's wife. This is how it happened:

We were going to Florida for a wedding and my uncle's wife could not go with us. She was going to join us there later. So we left for Florida, and on our way there, I had a vision of many people drowning and of a white coffin. I started feeling terrible in my stomach and I continued to have the vision over and over again. I didn't tell anyone about it and kept it to myself.

We got to Florida, and went to the wedding the next day. After the wedding, we went to my aunt's house and partied all night! But I still thought of that vision in my head.

The following day we went to pick up my uncle's wife at the train station. We got the others and went to the beach. Everyone was eager to get into the water, except for me. Something told me not to go in, but eventually I ignored it and went in with the others. Then, all of a sudden, we were drowning… !!!! We were crying for help, but no one came. I have no idea how I got out, but I did. All who were drowning managed to get out safely, except for one person. It was my uncle's wife, Anita Lake Rojas.

She was twenty-eight years old and left behind two beautiful children named Stephen and Carlos. It was a real shock for us.

Our plans to stay in Florida were changed from this sudden death. We spent that week in grief, depression, and sorrow. It was hard for us in the sense that we were the last to see her alive, but we were not her family.

I was not very close to Anita, but she did take my cousins and me out to the mall and to her parent's house. She and

44

her family were very sweet and her family still is. I think she was too young to die, but that was God's decision.

I feel kind of guilty because I saw this happen in my vision. I could have saved her. Sometimes I wish that it was me who died and not her. But I have learned that it wasn't my vision that made this happen. It was God's decision.

We really miss her and wish God would bring her back to us. We love you Anita!

Listening to Mongo Santamaría Calling the Spirits from Buffalo

by Olga Mendell

Mongo's hands are flying on the drum,
opening a path of air
for their bare black feet
their polished soles.

His voice is calling
for Obatalá,
King of spirits,
ruler of the white parts of the body,
for Osaín,
the great healer,
who smokes cigars and sometimes lives
inside a turtle shell,
for Changó,
who gallops his horse across the sky
and loves corn meal and red wine.

Mongo is calling Ochún,
queen of sweetness,
drinker of chamomile tea with honey,
the goddess no one has ever seen cry.
He is opening a path
for Yemayá, black as coal,
mother of the world,
immense and pure as the sea,
holding her fan of peacock feathers.

The spirits pass through
with their brilliant bead necklaces,

their cowrie shells
and pieces of divining dry coconut.
They don't see that it is snowing
in Buffalo,
they wear no coats, no shoes.

from Intaglio

Amanda

by Roberta Fernández

I

Transformation was definitely her speciality, and out of georgettes, piques, peaux de soie, organzas, shantungs and laces she made exquisite gowns adorned with delicate opaline beadwork which she carefully touched up with the thinnest slivers of iridescent cording that one could find. At that time I was so captivated by Amanda's creations that often before I fell asleep, I would conjure up visions of her workroom where luminous whirls of *lentejuelas de conchanacar* would be dancing about, softly brushing against the swaying fabrics in various shapes and stages of completion. Then, amidst the colorful threads and iridescent fabrics shimmering in a reassuring rhythm, she would get smaller and smaller until she was only the tiniest of gray dots among the colors and lights, and slowly, slowly, the uninterrupted gentle droning of the magical Singer sewing machine and her mocking, whispering voice would both vanish into a silent, solid darkness.

By day, whenever I had the opportunity I loved to sit next to her machine, observing her hands guiding the movement of the fabrics. I was so moved by what I saw that she soon grew to intimidate me and I almost never originated conversation. Therefore, our only communication for long stretches of time was my obvious fascination with the changes that transpired before my watchful eyes. Finally she would look up at me through her gold-rimmed glasses and ask *"¿Te gusta, muchacha?"*

In response to my nod she would proceed to tell me familiar details about the women who would be showing off her finished costumes at the Black and White Ball or at some other such event.

Rambling on with the reassurance of someone who has given considerable thought to everything she says, Amanda would then mesmerize me even further with her provocative gossip about the men and women who had come to our area many years before. Then, as she tied a thread here and added a touch there, I would feel compelled to ask her a question or two as my flimsy contribution to our lengthy conversation.

With most people I chatted freely but with Amanda I seldom talked since I had the distinct feeling by the time I was five or six that in addition to other apprehensions I had about her, she felt total indifference towards me. "How can she be so inquisitive?" I was positive she would be saying to herself even as I persisted with another question.

When she stopped talking to concentrate fully on what she was doing I would gaze directly at her, admiring how beautiful she looked. Waves of defeat would overtake me, for the self containment that she projected behind her austere appearance made me think she would never take notice of me, while I loved everything about her. I would follow the shape of her head from the central part of her dark auburn hair pulled down over her ears to the curves of the bun she wore at the nape of her long neck. Day in and day out she wore a gray shirtwaist with a narrow skirt and elbow-length sleeves which made her seem even taller than she was. The front had tiny stitched-down vertical pleats and a narrow deep pocket in which she sometimes tucked her eyeglasses. A row of straight pins with big plastic heads ran down the front of her neckline and a yellow measuring tape hung around her neck. Like the rest of the relatives she seemed reassuringly permanent in the uniform she had created for herself.

Her day lasted from seven in the morning until nine in

49

the evening. During this time she could dash off in a matter of two or three days an elaborate wedding dress or a classically simple evening gown for someone's fifteen-year old party, which Verónica would then embroider. Her disposition did not require her to concentrate on any one outfit from start to finish and this allowed her to work on many at once. It also meant she had dresses everywhere, hanging from the edge of the doors, on a wall-to-wall bar suspended near the ceiling and on three or four tables where they would be carefully laid out.

Once or twice, she managed to make a hysterical bride late to her own wedding. In those hectic instances, Amanda would have the sobbing bride step inside her dress, then hold her breath while she sewed in the back zipper by hand. Somehow people did not seem to mind these occasional slipups, for they kept coming back, again and again, from Saltillo and Monterrey, from San Antonio and Corpus Christi, and a few even from far-off Dallas and Houston. Those mid-Texas socialites seem to enjoy practicing their very singular Spanish with Amanda who never once let on that she really did speak perfect English, and, only after they were gone, would she chuckle over her little joke with us.

As far as her other designs went, her initial basic dress pattern might be a direct copy from *Vogue* magazine or it could stem from someone's wildest fantasy. From then on, the creation was Amanda's and every one of her clients trusted the final look to her own discretion. The svelte Club Campestre set from Monterrey and Nuevo Laredo would take her to Audrey Hepburn and Grace Kelly movies to point out the outfits they wanted, just as their mothers had done with Joan Crawford and Katherine Hepburn movies. Judging from their expressions as they pirouetted before their image in their commissioned artwork, she never failed their expectations except perhaps for that occasional zipperless bride. She certainly never disappointed me as I sat in solemn and curious attention, peering into her face as I searched for some trace of how she had acquired her special powers.

For there was another aspect to Amanda which only we seemed to whisper about, in very low tones, and that was that Amanda was dabbling in herbs. Although none of us considered her a real *hechicera* or enchantress, we always had reservations about drinking or eating anything she gave us, and whereas no one ever saw the proverbial little figurines, we fully suspected she had them hidden somewhere, undoubtedly decked out as exact replicas of those who had ever crossed her in any way.

Among her few real friends were two old women who came to visit her by night, much to everyone's consternation, for those two only needed one quick stolen look to convince you they were more than amateurs. Librada and Soledad were toothless old women swathed in black or brown from head-to-toe and they carried their back sack filled with herbs and potions slung over their shoulder, just as *brujas* did in my books. They had a stare that seemed to go right through you, and you knew that no thought was secret from them if you let them look even once into your eyes.

One day, in the year when it rained without stopping for many days in a row and the puddles swelled up with more bubbles than usual, I found myself sitting alone in the screened-in porch admiring the sound of the fat rain-drops on the roof; suddenly I looked up to find Librada standing there in her dark brown shawl, softly knocking on the door.

"The lady has sent a message to your mother," she said while my heart thumped so loudly its noise scared me even further. I managed to tell her to wait there, by the door, while I went to call my mother. By the time mother came to check on the visitor, Librada was already inside, sitting on the couch, and since the message was that Amanda wanted mother to call one of her customers to relay some information, I was left alone with the old woman. I sat on the floor pretending to work on a jig-saw puzzle while I really observed Librada's every move. Suddenly she broke the silence asking me how old I was and when my next birthday would be. Before I could phrase any words, mother was back with a note for Amanda, and Librada was on her way. Sensing my tension mother suggested we go into the kitchen to make some good hot chocolate and to talk about what had just happened.

After I drank my cup, I came back to the porch, picked up one of my *Jack and Jill*'s and lay on the couch. Then, as I rearranged a cushion, my left arm slid on a slimy greenish-gray substance and I let out such a screech that mother was at my side in two seconds. Angry at her for having taken so long to come to my aid, I kept wiping my arm on the dress and screaming, "Look at what that *bruja* has done." She very, very slowly took off my dress and told me to go into the shower and to soap myself well. In the meantime she cleaned up the mess with newspapers and burned them outside by the old brick pond. As soon as I came out of the shower she puffed me up all over with her lavender-fragranced bath powder and for the rest of the afternoon we tried to figure out what the strange episode had meant. Nothing much happened to anyone in the family during the following wet days and mother insisted we forget the incident.

Only, I didn't forget it for a long time. On my next visit to Amanda's I described in detail what had happened. She dismissed the entire episode as though it weren't important, shrugging, "Poor Librada. Why are you blaming her for what happened to you?"

With that I went back to my silent observation, now suspecting she too was part of a complex plot I couldn't figure out. Yet, instead of making me run, incidents like these drew me more to her, for I distinctly sensed she was my only link to other exciting possibilities which were not part of the everyday world of the others. What they could be I wasn't sure of but I was so convinced of the hidden powers in that house that I always wore my scapular and made the sign of the cross before I stepped inside.

After the rains stopped and the moon began to change colors, I began to imagine a dramatic and eerie outfit which I hoped Amanda would create for me. Without discussing it with my sisters I made it more and more sinister and finally, when the frogs stopped croaking, I built up enough nerve to ask her about it. "Listen, Amanda, could you make me the most beautiful outfit in the world? One that a witch would give her favorite daughter? So horrible that it would enchant everyone...maybe black with wings on it like a bat's."

She looked at me with surprise. "Why would you want such a thing?"

"Cross my heart and hope to die, I really won't try to scare anyone."

"*Pues, chulita,* I'm so busy right now, there's no way I can agree to make you anything. One of these days, when God decides to give me some time, I might consider it, but until then, I'm not promising anyone anything."

And then I waited. Dog days came and went, and finally when the white owl flew elsewhere I gave up on my request, brooding over my having asked for something I should have known would not be coming. Therefore the afternoon that Verónica dropped off a note saying that *la señora* wanted to see me that night because she had a surprise for me, I coolly said I'd be there only if my mother said I could go.

II

All the time I waited to be let in, I was very aware that I had left my scapular at home. I knew this time that something very special was about to happen to me, since I could see even from out there that Amanda had finally made me my very special outfit. Mounted on a little-girl dress-dummy, a swaying black satin cape was awaiting my touch. It was ankle-length with braided frogs cradling tiny buttons down to the knee. On the inside of the neckline was a black fur trim. "Cat fur," she confessed, and it tickled my neck as she buttoned the cape on me. The puffy sleeves fitted very tightly around the wrist, and on the upper side of each wristband was attached a cat's paw which hung down to my knuckles. Below the collar, on the left side of the cape, was a small stuffed heart in burgundy-colored velveteen and, beneath the heart, she had sewn-in red translucent beads.

As she pulled the rounded ballooning hood on me, rows of stitched-down pleats made it fit close to the head. Black chicken feathers framed my face, almost down to my eyes. Between the appliques of feathers, tiny bones were strung which gently touched my cheeks. The bones came from the sparrows which the cats had killed out in the garden, she reassured me. She then suggested I walk around the room so she could take a good look at me.

As I moved, the cat's paws rubbed against my hands and the bones of the sparrows bounced like what I imagined snowflakes would feel like on my face. Then she slipped a necklace over my head that was so long it reached down to my waist. It too was made of bones of sparrows strung on the finest glittering black thread, with little bells inserted here and there. I raised my arms and danced around the room, and the bells sounded sweet and clear in the silence. I glided about the room, then noticed in the mirror that Librada was sitting in the next room, laughing under her breath. Without thinking, I walked up to her and asked what she thought of my cape.

"Nenita, you look like something out of this world. Did you notice I just blessed myself? It scares me to think of the effect you are going to have on so many. *¡Que Dios nos libre!*"

I looked at Librada eye-to-eye for the first time, then felt that the room was not big enough to hold all the emotion inside of me. So I put my arms around Amanda and kissed her two, three, four times, then dramatically announced that I was going to show this most beautiful of all creations to my mother. I rushed outside hoping not to see anyone on the street and since luck was to be my companion for a brief while, I made it home without encountering a soul. Pausing outside the door of the kitchen where I could hear voices I took a deep breath, knocked as loudly as I could and in one simultaneous swoop, opened the door and stepped inside, arms outstretched as feathers, bones and *cascabeles* fluttered in unison with my heart.

After the initial silence, my sisters started to cry almost hysterically, and while my father turned to comfort them, my mother came towards me with a face I had never seen on her before. She breathed deeply, then quietly said I must never wear that outfit again. Since her expression frightened me somewhat, I took off the cape, mumbling under my breath over and over how certain people couldn't see special powers no matter how much they might be staring them in the face.

I held the *bruja* cape in my hands, looking at the tiny holes pierced through the bones of sparrows, then felt the points of the nails on the cat's paws. As I fingered the beads under the heart I knew that on that very special night when the green lights of the fire flies were flickering more brightly than usual, on that calm transparent night of nights I would soon be sleeping in my own witch's daughter's cape.

III

Sometime after the Judases were all aflame and spirals of light were flying everywhere, I slowly opened my eyes to a full moon shining on my face. Instinctively my hand reached to my neck and I rubbed the back of my fingers gently against the cat's fur. I should go outside I thought. Then I slipped off the bed and tip-toed to the back door in search of that which was not inside.

For a long time I sat on a lawn chair, rocking myself against its back, all the while gazing at the moon and the familiar surroundings which glowed so luminously within the vast universe while out there in the darkness, the constant chirping of the crickets and the cicadas reiterated the reassuring permanence of everything around me. None of us is allowed to relish in powers like that for long though, and the vision of transcendence exploded in a scream as two hands grabbed me at the shoulders then shook me back and forth. "What are you doing out here? Didn't I tell you to take off that awful thing?"

Once again I looked at my mother in defiance but immediately sensed that she was apprehensive rather than angry and I knew it was hopeless to argue with her. Carefully I undid the tiny rounded black buttons from the soft, braided loops and took off the cape for what I felt would be the last time.

IV

Years passed, much faster than before, and I had little time left for dark brown-lavender puddles and fanciful white owls in the night. Nor did I see my cape after that lovely-but-so-sad, once-in-a-lifetime experience of perfection in the universe. In fact, I often wondered if I had not invented that episode as I invented many others in those endless days of exciting and unrestrained possibilities.

Actually, the memory of the cape was something I tried to flick away on those occasions when the past assumed the unpleasantness of an uninvited but persistent guest; yet, no matter how much I tried, the intrusions continued. They were especially bothersome one rainy Sunday afternoon when all the clocks had stopped working one after another as though they too had wanted to participate in the tedium of the moment. So as not to remain still, I mustered all the energy I could and decided to pass the hours by poking around in the boxes and old trunks in the store-room.

Nothing of interest seemed to be the order of the afternoon when suddenly I came upon something wrapped in yellowed tissue paper. As I unwrapped the package, I uttered a sigh of surprise on discovering that inside was the source of the disturbances I had been trying to avoid. I cried as I fingered all the details on the little cape, for it was as precious as it had been on the one day I had worn it many years before. Only the fur had stiffened somewhat from the dryness in the trunk.

Once again I marvelled at Amanda's gifts. The little black cape was so obviously an expression of genuine love that it seemed a shame it had been hidden for all those years. I carefully lifted the cape out of the trunk wondering why my mother had not burned it as she had threatened, yet knowing full well why she had not.

V

From then on I placed the little cape among my collection of few but very special possessions which accompanied me everywhere I went. I even had a stuffed dummy made, upon which I would arrange the cape in a central spot in every home I made. Over the years, the still-crisp little cape ripened in meaning, for I could not imagine anyone ever again taking the time to create anything as personal for me as Amanda had done when our worlds had coincided for a brief and joyous period in those splendid days of luscious white gardenias.

When the end came I could hardly bear it. It happened many years ago when the suitcase containing the little cape got lost en route on my first trip west. No one could understand why the loss of something as quaint as a black cape with chicken feathers, bones of sparrows and cat's paws could cause anyone to carry on in such a manner. Their lack of sympathy only increased my own awareness of what was gone, and for months after I first came to these foggy coastal shores I would wake up to *lentejuelas de conchanacar* whirling about in the darkness, just as they had done so long ago in that magical room in Amanda's house.

VI

Back home, Amanda is aging well, and although I haven't seen her in years, lately I have been dreaming once again about the enchantment which her hands gave to everything they touched, especially when I was very tiny and to celebrate our birthdays, my father, she and I had a joint birthday party lasting three days. During this time, he would use bamboo sticks to make a skeletal frame for a kite, and then Amanda would take the frame and attach thin layers of marquisette to it with angel cords. In the late afternoon, my father would hold on to the cords, while I floated about on the kite above the shrubs and bushes; and it was all such fun. I cannot recall the exact year when those celebrations stopped, nor what we did with all those talismanic presents but I must remember to sort through all the trunks and boxes in my mother's storeroom the next time that I am home.

In the Family

by María Elena Llano

When my mother found out that the large mirror in the living room was inhabited, we all gradually went from disbelief to astonishment, and from this to a state of contemplation, ending up by accepting it as an everyday thing.

The fact that the old, spotted mirror reflected the dear departed in the family was not enough to upset our lifestyle. Following the old saying of "let the house burn as long as no one sees the smoke," we kept the secret to ourselves since, after all, it was nobody else's business.

At any rate, some time went by before each one of us would feel absolutely comfortable about sitting down in our favorite chair and learning that, in the mirror, that same chair was occupied by somebody else. For example, it could be Aurelia, my grandmother's sister (1939), and even if cousin Natalie would be on my side of the room, across from her would be the almost forgotten Uncle Nicholas (1927). As could have been expected, our departed reflected in the mirror presented the image of a family gathering almost identical to our own, since nothing, absolutely nothing in the living room—the furniture and its arrangement, the light, etc.—was changed in the mirror. The only difference was that on the other side it was them instead of us.

I don't know about the others, but I sometimes felt that, more than a vision in the mirror, I was watching an old worn-out movie, already clouded. The deceaseds' efforts to copy our gestures were slower, restrained, as if the mirror were not truly showing a direct image but the reflection of some other reflection.

From the very beginning I knew that everything would get more complicated as soon as my cousin Clara got back from vacation. Because of her boldness and determination,

Clara had long given me the impression that she had blundered into our family by mistake. This suspicion had been somewhat bolstered by her being one of the first women dentists in the country. However, the idea that she might have been with us by mistake went away as soon as my cousin hung up her diploma and started to embroider sheets beside my grandmother, aunts and other cousins, waiting for a suitor who actually did show up but was found lacking in one respect or another—nobody ever really found out why.

Once she graduated, Clara became the family oracle, even though she never practiced her profession. She would prescribe painkillers and was the arbiter of fashion; she would choose the theater shows and rule on whether the punch had the right amount of liquor at each social gathering. In view of all this, it was fitting that she take one month off every year to go to the beach.

That summer when Clara returned from her vacation and learned about my mother's discovery, she remained pensive for a while, as if weighing the symptoms before issuing a diagnosis. Afterwards, without batting an eye, she leaned over the mirror, saw for herself that it was true, and then tossed her head, seemingly accepting the situation. She immediately sat by the bookcase and craned her neck to see who was sitting in the chair on the other side. "Gosh, look at Gus," was all she said. There in the very same chair the mirror showed us Gus, some sort of godson of Dad, who after a flood in his hometown came to live with us and had remained there in the somewhat ambiguous character of adoptive poor relation. Clara greeted him amiably with a wave of the hand, but he seemed busy, for the moment, with something like a radio tube and did not pay attention to her. Undoubtedly, the mirror people weren't going out of their way to be sociable. This must have wounded Clara's self-esteem, although she did not let it on.

Naturally, the idea of moving the mirror to the dining

room was hers. And so was its sequel: to bring the mirror near the big table, so we could all sit together for meals.

In spite of my mother's fears that the mirror people would run away or get annoyed because of the fuss, everything went fine. I must admit it was comforting to sit every day at the table and see so many familiar faces, although some of those from the other side were distant relatives, and others, due to their lengthy—although unintentional—absence, were almost strangers. There were about twenty of us sitting at the table every day, and even if their gestures and movements seemed more remote than ours and their meals a little washed-out, we generally gave the impression of being a large family that got along well.

At the boundary between the real table and the other one, on this side, sat Clara and her brother Julius. On the other side was Eulalia (1949), the second wife of Uncle Daniel, aloof and indolent in life, and now the most distant of anyone on the other side. Across from her sat my godfather Sylvester (1952), who even though he was not a blood relative was always a soul relation. I was sad to see that Sylvester had lost his ruddiness, for he now looked like a faded mannequin, although his full face seemed to suggest perfect health. This pallor did not suit the robust Asturian, who undoubtedly felt a bit ridiculous in these circumstances.

For a while we ate all together, without further incidents or problems. We mustn't forget Clara, however, who we had allowed to sit at the frontier between the two tables, the equator separating what was from what was not. Although we paid no attention to the situation, we should have. Compounding our regrettable oversight was the fact that lethargic Eulalia sat across from her so that one night, with the same cordiality with which she had addressed Gus, Clara asked Eulalia to pass the salad. Eulalia affected the haughty disdain of offended royalty as she passed the spectral salad bowl, filled with dull lettuce and grayish semi-transparent tomatoes which Clara gobbled up, smiling mischievously at the novelty of it all. She watched us with the same defiance in her eyes that she had on the day she enrolled in a man's subject. There was no time to act. We just watched her grow pale, then her smile faded away until finally Clara collapsed against the mirror.

Once the funeral business was over and we sat back down at the table again, we saw that Clara had taken a place on the other side. She was between cousin Baltazar (1940) and a great-uncle whom we simply called "Ito."

This faux pas dampened our conviviality somewhat. In a way, we felt betrayed; we felt that they had grievously abused our hospitality. However, we ended up divided over the question of who was really whose guest. It was also plain that our carelessness and Clara's irrepressible inquisitiveness had contributed to the mishap. In fact, a short time later we realized that there wasn't a great deal of difference between what Clara did before and what she was doing now, and so we decided to overlook the incident and get on with things. Nevertheless, each day we became less and less sure about which side was life and which its reflection, and as one bad step leads to another, I ended up taking Clara's empty place.

I am now much closer to them. I can almost hear the distant rustle of the folding and unfolding of napkins, the slight clinking of glasses and cutlery, the movement of chairs. The fact is that I can't tell if these sounds come from them or from us. I'm obviously not worried about clearing that up. What really troubles me, though, is that Clara doesn't seem to behave properly, with either the solemnity or with the opacity owed to her new position; I don't know how to put it. Even worse, the problem is that I—more than anybody else in the family—may become the target of Clara's machinations, since we were always joined by a very special affection, perhaps because we were the same age and had shared the same children's games and the first anxieties of adolescence . . .

As it happens, she is doing her best to get my attention, and ever since last Monday she has been waiting for me to slip up so she can pass me a pineapple this big, admittedly a little bleached-out, but just right for making juice and also a bit sour, just as she knows I like it.

Translated by Beatriz Teleki

CHAPTER 3

LA FAMILIA

MAMACITA

by Judith Ortiz Cofer

Mamacita hummed all day long
over the caboose kitchen
of our railroad flat.
From my room I'd hear her *humm*,
No words slowed the flow
of Mamacita's soulful sounds;
it was *humm* over the yellow rice,
and *umm* over the black beans.
Up and down two syllables she'd climb
and slide—each note a task accomplished.
From chore to chore, she was the prima donna
in her daily operetta.
Mamacita's wordless song was her connection
to the oversoul,
her link with life,
her mantra,
a lifeline to her own Laughing Buddha,
as she dragged her broom
across a lifetime of linoleum floors.

So Much for Mañana

by Judith Ortiz Cofer

After twenty years in the mainland
Mother's gone back to the island
to let her skin
melt from her bones
under her native sun.
She no longer wears stockings,
girdles or tight clothing.
Brown as a coconut,
she takes siestas in a hammock,
and writes me letters that say:
"Stop chasing your own shadow, niña,
come down here and taste the piña,
put away those heavy books,
don't you worry about your shape,
here on the Island men look
for women who can carry a little weight.
On every holy day,
I burn candles and I pray
that your brain won't split
like an avocado pit
from all that studying.
What do you say?
Abrazos from your Mama and a blessing
from that saint, Don Antonio, el cura."
I write back: "Someday I will go back
to your Island and get fat,
but not now, Mamá, maybe mañana."

Elena

by Pat Mora

My Spanish isn't enough.
I remember how I'd smile
listening to my little ones,
understanding every word they'd say,
their jokes, their songs, their plots.
       Vamos a pedirle dulces a mamá. Vamos.
But that was in Mexico.
Now my children go to American high schools.
They speak English. At night they sit around
the kitchen table, laugh with one another.
I stand by the stove and feel dumb, alone.
I bought a book to learn English.
My husband frowned, drank more beer.
My oldest said, *"Mamá,* he doesn't want you
to be smarter than he is." I'm forty,
embarrassed at mispronouncing words,
embarrassed at the laughter of my children,
the grocer, the mailman. Sometimes I take
my English book and lock myself in the bathroom,
say the thick words softly,
for if I stop trying, I will be deaf
when my children need help.

La Rosa Mordida

by Rosa María Arenas

For My Mother
María Berta Arenas
Feb. 25, 1912-Feb. 7, 1984

When María Arenas was getting ready to leave
she came into our dreams to tell us.

When María Arenas was getting ready to leave
she saw the look on our faces and
considered how not to hurt us.
But since that was impossible
she came into our dreams to tell us.

"Be careful," she told her friend Socorro.
"I'm going away and I won't see you for a long time
but look what I brought."

A rose, a perfect rose
"Y mira que es bonita. Es verdad que es bonita."

And María Arenas bit
off the head of the perfect rose,
her tongue tasting bitter perfume,
her hand twisting the thorny stem.

La rosa mordida.

"That is how I feel," she said.
"Así, como la rosa.
Ten cuidado hijita. Ya me voy."

Six Take Away One

by Rosa Elena Yzquierdo

During the day Mom worked as a cook at Franklin Elementary. That was the year Dad was laid off, so she had to work. She'd move big boxes that contained 32 oz. cans of peas and beans; she cooked gallons of food—and of course helped clean the kitchen. She did a lot of things that women shouldn't do if they think they're pregnant.

There were five of us. I was the oldest, age twelve, and my youngest sister was seven. Mom knew she was going to have another baby, even though she hadn't been to the doctor. With Dad laid off and mom working as a cook, there wasn't enough money or time to rear another child.

"Look, I have something to show you."

"Mom, what is it?"

"I lost the baby."

"What baby—you're not even big—how do you know?"

She showed me the container, and in it was a little black circle surrounded by a filmy pink web.

"What do I do with it?" she asked.

"Flush it down the toilet," I said, and she did.

Mom was forty-one when that happened, and she still feels guilty. She wonders what it would have been like to have that baby.

"I think it was a boy," she says whenever we recall the afternoon.

She remembers how hard she worked and how broke we were and how busy she was taking care of us. But what she remembers most is knowing she was pregnant and thinking to herself, over and over, that she wouldn't have another baby—not again.

Dear Tía

by Carolina Hospital

I do not write.
The years have frightened me away.
My life in a land so familiarly foreign,
a denial of your presence.
Your name is mine.
One black and white photograph of your youth,
all I hold on to.
One story of your past.

The pain comes not from nostalgia.
I do not miss your voice urging me in play,
your smiles,
or your pride when others called you my mother.
I cannot close my eyes and feel your soft skin;
listen to your laughter;
smell the sweetness of your bath.
I write because I cannot remember at all.

Silence Within

by Sandra Orta

I would like to know him. He gave me life. To take him for granted wouldn't be wrong, then again, it wouldn't be right. I see him, but I don't visualize him in a way one would look at a person they once cherished. I'm holding back feelings that need to be shown. Telling him "I love you" would be covering up my true emotions and the burden would be too infinite for me to handle alone.

The feelings I have for him are silenced because he does not know me, nor does he seem to care to know me. I've tried to get my priorities straight. I know they say love takes time to prosper, but too much time apart can make love fade.

He represents a vague characterization of a man who abandoned me physically as well as mentally, and to call him "father" would be a great step for me that I'm not yet willing to accept. I haven't broken through the silence within me, and until he approaches me with the feelings I crave to receive, the silence within me will grow and grow.

Now that I have expressed my silence on paper, I feel a heavy load has just been lifted and I am able to handle the anger and sorrow I carry within myself. Although I've tried to express my emotions, no one will really know how stable the silence has kept itself and how bad I want it to be broken. But another part of me wants to be silenced because the risk of being denied again would be too great a downfall for me.

Thoughts that were wandering around in my head are now sketched out on paper. To get this far has been a great challenge.

Abuela

by Denise Alcalá

Sing on
blue eyes, sparkle
in crinkling crevices
sing on
worn hands, continuous
in their motion
sing on
sturdy legs, dancing
against age, time
sing on
sing on
with head
thrown back
lips forever quivering
and heart rolling forth
sing on
to empty
walls
to beds and buses
guadalajara
will be nothing
without you

Abuela

by Rosa Elena Yzquierdo

My abuela begins her daily ritual with "Santa María, madre de Dios . . ." She goes outside and waters the trailing plants surrounding the nickety old fence. Yerbas are growing profusely in Folger's coffee cans and an old Motorola. Abuela comes back inside and mixes flour, salt, and shortening to make tortillas for me. One of the tortillas cooking on the comal fills with air.

"That means you're going to get married," she says, then continues to knead and cook each tortilla with care, making sure to bless the first one of the stack.

"Abuela, I had a dream about fleas. What does that mean?"

"It means you're going to get some money, mija."

"Abuela, my stomach hurts."

"¿Te doy un tesito mija?"

She picks the yerbas, prepares them, and makes a tea for me. No smell to it, but it tastes like milk of magnesia—maybe worse.

"Drink this tea every morning for nine days before breakfast, and your stomach-aches will disappear for one year."

She has always said to me, "Remember your dreams because they have special meaning. Remember the yerbas that grow in the wild, how they work, when to use them. Remember the cures for evil eye, fright, and fever.

"Sweep the herbs across the body and repeat three apostle's creeds to drive out evil spirits. Crack an egg in a glass of water and say three Hail Marys to take away evil eye and fever. Remember these things. They are all a part of you—a part of your heritage."

She said once, "Yo soy mexicana; tu mama es mexicana pero tú eres americana."

I just try to hold on.

MENTE JOVEN:

nothin' like a pensive child

by Evangelina Vigil-Piñón

mente joven: nothin' like a pensive child,
cold north wind flapping against his hair
and tender face

and you remember grandpa—
"Papá," le decían todos
when he died
you were only age six
and you recall parientes
making you walk up to the corpse
and kiss its cold face and you
remember, too, how he used
to terrorize you into "un besito"
on his brown, leathersoft face
made rough by salt-and-pepper beard,
you so scared of him, whom you
hardly ever saw—
he'd prop you up and sit you on his lap,
you frozen stiff with shyness and embarassment
and he asking you things and you
not knowing how or what to answer
only that he was so desconocido
yet full of so much love
and so big and brown and strong
"salúdele a su abuelito," te decían
and you recall how he would
always give you a bright shiny penny
pa' comprar un chicle en el molino next door
maybe you might get un premio!

A Man So Special

by Enike Smith

I could feel the steam coming from the sidewalk through my white skippies. I was hoping they would open the hydrant so I could cool my tired feet. I had been walking all day. My mom had taken me and my baby sister, Angie, to Central park for a picnic. It had gotten so hot towards noon that we decided to leave.

Walking back towards home I saw my uncle Héctor. Uncle Héctor was a big man with broad shoulders. He was a construction worker until last year when he retired. I remember when I was little he used to pick me and my cousin Antonio up over his shoulder. He used to roar and call us his Little Hijos. I remember I used to laugh, as my cousin gasped for air (he had asthma).

Héctor is sixty-five now, ten years older than my dad. He walks with a limp — he was shot three months ago when there was a drug shootout in the subway. I remember it was all over the news. My uncle was so proud, not about being shot, but that he had caught the guy selling the drugs.

Now he walked down the street with his smooth wooden cane. He had on his favorite blue Yankee baseball cap. His jeans were faded from having been washed hundreds of times. He wore a clean white T-shirt. He greeted us with a large smile, gave my mother a kiss on the cheek, and lifted me off the ground. "You're getting heavy, little Juanita, you been drinking too much milk." He put me down slowly and straightened up. "You're going to have to start keeping this girl in the house, María, she's becoming quite a looker. There will be boys coming any minute now, you wait and see." He let out a big laugh.

"Oh, Héctor, the boys are already coming. Last week she got a call from this boy . . . I can't seem to remember his . . ."

"Ma!"

"Pepito — that's what his name was — I'm so bad at remembering names." She let out a little laugh and picked up Angie.

"Oh, well, excuuuuuse me!!" He shook his hips and gave me a little smile.

"Well we got to get home, it's boiling out here," my mother said taking a tissue out of her pocket with her free hand.

"Like Puerto Rico, ah," he gave my mother a little nudge.

"Except there's no shade, no big trees." He rubbed his moustache. "I really miss it, it's been about . . . what, twenty years? I still can remember it as if it was yesterday."

"I do too, but this is where we are now."

I hated when my parents and my uncle got to talking about Puerto Rico. I had never been there, but they got all misty eyed when they talked about it, like it was heaven or something.

"Well, let me get these kids out of the sun. Héctor, dinner at our house tonight, chicken and potato salad."

"What happened to rice and beans? I expect a Puerto Rican dinner when I go to a Puerto Rican household."

"Well, Héctor, then you're going to have to go somewhere else to eat." My mom let out a little laugh.

"You Americans, God, so cold." My mom hit him lightly on the arm and gave him a kiss on the cheek.

We got home about an hour later. My dad was lounging on the couch watching *La Intrusa*. "Got you hooked, ha! You are a pitiful excuse of a man watching this trash."

"I was turning the channel, and this just happened to be on. There's nothing else on anyway." My father was defending himself very badly. "Okay, I confess, I did it and I'll do it again." He stood up and gave my mother a kiss on the cheek.

"You've been watching too much TV, Carlos. Where's ma?"

"Where she always is, in her room in front of the television."

"Dios mío, my God, she never leaves that room of hers."

She walked to the back of the house. "Ma, Ma, come out of there. I want to talk to you — come out here." I could hear the door open.

"Qué tú quieres? What do you want? I'm watching *La Intrusa*, come back later." The door shut again.

"That woman, she only comes outside to eat and read the paper." My mom sat down at the table. The door in the back of the house opened slowly, and my grandmother walked out sliding her cane along the floor.

"What do you want, María, is it time to eat yet? Oh my God, look at Angie. She's filthy, don't you clean this child?" She took Angie by the hand and led her into the bathroom. "We are going to clean you up." I could hear the water running.

"Carlos, Héctor's coming to dinner tonight, I don't want you staying up all hours of the night. You men don't stop talking till at least one a.m. We have church tomorrow, and I want to get there early so we can get a seat close to Padre Santiago." Carlos let out a little laugh.

"And where is it written that men must talk the night away? Tonight lights out at eleven o'clock," he screamed from the living room.

My mom turned and headed towards the kitchen. "Chicken and potato salad tonight. Juanita, come and peel these potatoes." It was strange, all of a sudden my mother had gotten into cooking American dishes from this new book she bought called *3000 Ways to Cook an American Dish*. Yesterday we had pork chops.

It wasn't until eight o'clock that we got a phone call. I answered the phone. The voice was unfamiliar. "Hello, is this Mr. Ruiz? Hello?" I fell silent.

"Daddy, the phone, I don't know who it is." I felt tears swelling up in my eyes, I knew something had to be wrong.

"Hello, this is Mr. Ruiz . . . okay . . . uh-huh . . . okay, we'll come down." He hung up the phone. "María, we got to go down to the hospital. Héctor had a heart attack." He went into the closet and got his jacket. "He's at Mount Sinai."

"Papi can I go?" I pleaded with him for five minutes until he opened the door.

"Okay, get your sweater, it's starting to get cooler." I ran to my room and got my sweater.

We took the Number 6 train to the hospital. When we got there, there was a nurse sitting at the desk. "Please, can I have the room number of Héctor Ruiz, please." She typed something on the computer.

"Room 301, but she can't go up, she's too young. How old are you little girl?" She stood up and stared at me.

"She's fourteen, can we go now?" She gave us two passes and sent us upstairs.

My uncle lay there. He looked like he was dead. I never saw him like this before. He looked so pale and weak. I was used to him letting out his big roaring laugh every time we met him . . . but not this time. He didn't fling me up in the air and say, "how is my Little Hija." He just lay there. It felt like my stomach had just done a flying leap.

My mom went over to him and started talking to him. "Héctor, it's me and Carlos, and Juanita. We brought you some chicken." Uncle Héctor didn't wake up, he didn't even move to show he knew we were there. My mom cried, and my dad gently moved her toward the chair near the door.

"I think we better leave. Come on Juanita." I couldn't move, I don't know why, but I couldn't move. "Juanita, come on, we're going." He grabbed me by my arm. I cried.

When we got home, I fell asleep softly beside my sister, but I woke up crying the next morning. I saw my mom sitting still on the couch, and my dad pacing the living room floor. My mother spoke in a whisper, her voice shaking. "I don't know what to do Carlos, I just don't know what to do."

"He's dead isn't he? Isn't he?" I shouted at them accusingly. "Will someone answer me?" I wiped the tears from my face.

"Yes he's dead, I'm sorry baby." I ran into my mother's arms, and she held me as I cried.

I stood near the coffin. My uncle looked so still, as if he were alive. I wanted to run over to him and tell him to wake up. I thought any second now he would jump and say, "Fooled you, didn't I," and everyone would laugh, and then we'd all go home and eat the big dinner that my mother had prepared. But he didn't. He just lay there, eyes closed, in the same suit he had worn to my elementary school graduation.

I could never forget him, I will never forget him. He will always be the man who could pick me up with one hand and call me his Little Hija. He will always be someone special to me.

CHRISTMAS WAS A TIME OF PLENTY

by Nicholasa Mohr

Compared to the rest of the year, Christmas was a time of plenty when I was a child. That was saying a great deal for me and my six older brothers. We were the children of Puerto Rican migrants, living in New York City at the height of the Great Depression. Where and how my parents and the older folks were to get money for Christmas each and every year depended on "un milagro," "God's mercy," or "just plain luck."

At the beginning of World War II, and just before my older brothers left for the Armed Forces, we were all still home. I was quite young, but I can still remember the electricity that permeated the air at Christmas time. My parents together with aunts and uncles would purchase a large sow from the local butcher. They would carefully spice and fix that sow in the traditional Puerto Rican manner. Then, it was sent to an "out of town" bakery . . . a place far from where we lived on 105th Street and Madison Avenue, called Queens. The reason was that no one had an oven large enough to roast the sow. It was delivered to us hot and ready to serve on Christmas Eve, which was when we had our celebration. Traditional dishes like arroz con gandules (seasoned rice with tiny, dry, green peas and pork), pasteles (delicate meat pies, made from root plants and plantains), and rice pudding were also served. I thought that the building itself would surely elevate to heaven just from the sheer goodness and delight of all of those flavors floating and steaming around in the atmosphere.

We all got ready to party by piling the living room furniture into the small bedrooms, making room for wooden kegs of beer and creating a dance floor. We also cleared an easy path to and from the kitchen.

That entire night and into the early hours of the morning, friends and neighbors would come into our home, eat and visit. Some brought their guitars and their accordions; others recited poetry. Speeches were made to the effect that we should all unite and help win this terrible war that was threatening all of mankind. Prayers were offered asking God to be on our side against the enemy and protect our young men, who would have to leave home. In between the speeches, prayers and entertainment, our record player sounded out all the latest Latin hits, including patriotic war songs. "PON PON CAYO EL JAPON . . . PIN PIN CAYO BERLIN" was a favorite.

The younger children like myself fell asleep sooner than the others. We were bedded down in one of the overcrowded bedrooms. Exhausted and happy, we slept soundly, oblivious to the noise and excitement in the other rooms. We were too busy dreaming of the special brand-new toys that might be waiting for us under the brightly lit, tinsel-trimmed, Christmas tree. I hoped this year the adults would be more generous with the gifts I wanted, instead of the practical sweater or the woolen knee socks needed for school.

The next day and for about a week we ate Christmas food without worrying about asking for seconds. Then one day it was over. The Christmas tree was undressed and thrown out, its fate, to be burned in the street. Later we all watched the warm blaze illuminate the cold winter night. Once more we were reminded of the lean times, the daily monotony of school and getting to bed early.

Soon my four oldest brothers went into the service to fight in the second World War. We at home were issued ration books for meat, milk, clothing and other items.

There were good times in between the hard years that followed; some of us moved far away; others died. Most of us just grew up.

Many years went by before we could all manage to get together once more at Christmas time. When we did, everyone could still recall almost vividly those magical Christmases back then . . . in our urban village set in the heart of New York City.

CHAPTER 4

RECUERDO: MEMORIES FROM CHILDHOOD

This Morning There Were Rainbows in the Sprinklers

by Lorna Dee Cervantes

This morning
there were rainbows in the sprinklers.
My hollow heels clopped as they wore away the pavement
Clop, clop, clop.
I sang a worn out folk song
to the steady clop of my heels
wearing out the song
along with my heels
along with the pavement.
I was glad
because I wasn't sleepy anymore
but I yawned
more out of habit than out of sleepiness.
Today it's spring
and the remnants of April crush against my skin
in the wind.
It feels good.
The sky is clear
and I can see last night's quarter moon
like it was etched in the sky with cloud dust.
I time out my song to end
just as I reach my destiny.
I feel like I'm in a movie
a musical
with someone else walking down the street singing too.
I wait to see how the plot ends
because it's my story
and I choose the cast
and I'm directing.

87

REMOLINO EN MI TAZA

by Evangelina Vigil-Piñón

I love to spill a splash
of thick white cream
into a delicious steaming cup
of grandma's strong strong black coffee
swirl some sweet
and then anticipatingly
hot kiss
the spinning wheel of brown fortune
to a soothing tasty
stop

ESPERANZA

by Nicholasa Mohr

August, 1941

Nilda had said good-bye to her mother at Grand Central Station and, now on board the train, she wondered what life would be like away from her family and the Barrio. The train was headed for Upstate New York, not New Jersey as she had told Petra. This was the first time she had ever been without her family and out of her neighborhood on her own. She looked around and up and down the train car and saw a bunch of kids, none of whom she recognized. The nuns sat in pairs, staring straight ahead and not speaking.

Slowly, then rapidly, the city began to fade from view as Nilda looked out the window. First, the Park Avenue Market began to disappear and she looked back at 110th Street where she went shopping with her mother almost every day; then all the buildings, tenements, streetlights, and traffic faded from view. Panic seized her and she swallowed, fighting a strong urge to cry as she longed to go back home that very second.

She saw large sections of trees and grass interspersed with small houses. Once in a while a group of cows behind barbed wire would come into view. "Look, cows!" "Wow, those are real cows!" some of the kids cried out. Nilda strained her neck, trying to get a good view of the animals as the train whizzed by. Once they saw some horses. The ride took them past many little houses, most painted white, some with picket fences surrounded by trees and grass. There were no tall buildings at all. Small white churches with pointed steeples. Large barns and weather vanes. Neat patches of grass and flowers. It reminded her of the movies. Like the Andy Hardy pictures, she almost said out loud. In those movies Mickey Rooney and his whole family were always so happy. They lived in a whole house all for themselves. She started thinking about all those houses that so swiftly passed by the train window. Families and kids, problems that always had happy endings. A whole mess of happiness, she thought, just laid out there before my eyes. It didn't seem real, yet here was the proof because people really lived in those little houses. Recalling a part of the movie where Mickey Rooney goes to his father the judge for advice, Nilda smiled, losing herself in the happy plot of the story.

"Don't pick your nose," snapped a nun. "You'll get worms." Nilda looked around her as if she had just awakened. "You! You! I'm talking to you." She realized that the nun was pointing to her and she could feel the embarrassment spreading all over her face as everyone laughed.

At the train depot they all boarded several buses and after a short ride arrived at their destination. The children were all lined up in different groups according to sex and age. Nilda stood in line with the rest of the girls in her group. She looked about her and saw several ugly grey buildings skirted by water. The day was gloomy, adding to the bleakness of the place, which looked like an abandoned factory.

The children stood about in their assigned groups as the nuns and brothers cautioned them to silence. Other children were walking about near the buildings; obviously there were some campers here already. Nilda thought, they don't look so happy to me. Someone blew a whistle. "All right now, let's march!" said a brother, waving his arm and pointing towards one of the buildings. He wore rimless glasses and his red hair was slicked down.

"Let's follow Brother Sean, everyone," said one of the nuns. There was a dank smell coming from the water. Nilda noticed a thin layer of oily film covering the water near the shoreline. She walked along with the other children towards one of the buildings. The gritty sand under her feet stank of oil.

They were led into a very large room with long wooden tables and benches. Everywhere Nilda looked there was a crucifix or a holy statue. Each group was assigned a table to sit at. A nervous chatter was beginning among the children. A large red-faced nun walked up and clapped her hands vigorously. "Silence, silence now, children. Let me introduce Father Shaw. He will explain everything you want to know. Now," she looked at the group seriously, "I expect complete quiet and your undivided attention when Father Shaw speaks." With that she stepped aside and an even larger red-faced priest with a pinkish bald head began to speak.

"Thank you, sister." He paused, looking at the rows of tables and benches filled with children, and said, "Now, I want to see all those lucky faces. Why lucky? I can tell you why! You have been fortunate enough to leave the hot city behind. How many kids do you know that can leave the city? We intend to have a good time, of course. But every one of us is obligated to show our Savior Jesus Christ our thanks by living, behaving, and thinking like good Catholics. Not just at Mass. Here we carry it through every moment. Now, how many of you have made your First Communion?"

Most of the children eagerly picked up their hands. Nilda put her hands on her lap. Although she would be ten years old in a couple of months, she had never received Communion. "Well, that's wonderful!" Father Shaw said. "For those children who have not received Communion yet, we will have a special religious instruction group every day. They will have a chance to catch up on Catechism." His smile faded. "Rules are to be obeyed here. We deal with no nonsense. Let me warn everyone, especially the smart alecks, that any kind of misbehavior will be dealt with so that it doesn't happen a second time. We want no Judas or Jew!"

91

Pausing, he then asked, smiling with humor, "Are there any here, by the way?" The large nun was the first to laugh, bringing giggles and cries of "Noooooo" from the children.

Nilda thought of her stepfather's constant blasphemy and his many arguments with her mother, as he attacked the Catholic Church. I wish I could tell Papa, she thought. He might just convince Mama to let me go back home right now, even before I have to open my suitcase.

In that same large room with the long wooden tables and benches, campers were fed their meals. Supper that night consisted of first, a clear soup, which was so tasteless that it took Nilda a while to recognize the flavor—it was chicken— then the main course, a sausage pie. The meat was wrapped in a soft dough having the consistency of oatmeal; it was served with creamed beets and grits, bread spread with jam, and a glass of powdered milk. Dessert was stewed plums and prunes in a heavy syrup. Nilda was not very hungry.

One of the sisters walked up and down between the tables, watching the children. "Here we eat what's put on our plates. We don't waste food. That's a sin! There are many less fortunate children who go hungry in Europe and all over the world." Nilda felt a sharp poke in her left shoulder blade. The nun was standing behind her. "You can do better than that, now." Before she could turn around to look, the nun had walked over to another girl. "Eat what you have on your plate, young lady, because that's all you get until breakfast. I don't want to hear that anybody's hungry tonight." Looking down at her food, Nilda put some of it on her fork and shoved it into her mouth. She tried not to think, as she chewed, of her mother and the good-tasting food she had at home.

A gong sounded. The sister clapped her hands. "All right, now just a minute, stay in your seats." She walked around inspecting the children's plates. "Well, we're going to overlook some of these full plates tonight because this is this

92

group's first day here. Tomorrow we expect all the plates to be completely clean. Let's line up." The girls in Nilda's section left the tables and formed a line two abreast.

A young nun walked up to the group of girls. "I'm Sister Barbara," she said smiling. "Follow me, girls, and please no talking." She led them out of the building and over to the dormitory where Nilda had previously put her suitcase. The building was very much like the others, two stories high, the outside concrete and brick. Inside, the walls were painted a dark color; the paint was peeling and large cracks were visible on the walls and ceiling.

The group of children walked along into the dormitory, a very large room with rows of army cots all made up. Army khaki blankets were neatly tucked in the cots. Each cot had a pillow with a white pillowcase and at the end of the cot was a footlocker. Sister Barbara turned, still smiling, and said, "Shower time. Get your robes and towels, pajamas and toothbrushes. We have a nice full day tomorrow and it's time to get ready for bed." Nilda looked out; it was still light outside. She thought, Man, at home I could go outside and play with Petra and little Benji.

"Leave your clothes on, girls. We have to go to another building," said the smiling nun.

Sister Barbara led the group outside and into another similar building only one story high. Nilda looked at the long room with benches lined against one side of the wall and showers lining the other side. She could see the toilets in the next room; none of them had doors, just toilets lined up next to each other. The girls started to undress. Nilda felt a little embarrassed, naked with all those girls she hardly knew. Some of the others were already under the showers. "Ooooooooh, it's cold." "Ayeeeee, it's freezing."

"Now, girls, we're a little short of hot water so just go in and come out quickly, that's all," said Sister Barbara, all smiling and pleasant. Feeling the goose bumps all over her body, Nilda jumped in and out, drying herself and getting her pajamas and robe on. "Anyone who has to go to the john, go now." A few girls walked into the next room. "You cannot go later, now is the time, before we get to bed." Nilda was glad she had peed in the shower, and so she stayed put.

Back in the dormitory, Nilda noticed some food carts lined up against the side wall. They were all full of large bottles of Phillips' Milk of Magnesia. Set at the side of the bottles were tiny glasses that looked like the whiskey glasses they had at home for parties and Christmastime. Grabbing a cart by the handles, Sister Barbara started walking, pushing the cart over to the section where Nilda was. Still smiling and in a soft voice, she said to one of the girls, "It's time for our laxative." She handed the glass to the girl. The girl did not respond; she sat there looking at the nun.

"How is it going?" a loud voice said. Nilda saw the same large nun who had introduced Father Shaw earlier that day. "They are taking their laxatives, aren't they? I hope no one here is a baby and has to be treated like one." Both women were now standing over the girl. Nilda watched as the older larger woman took the small glass out of the younger nun's hand and shoved it right up to the girl's face. The girl grabbed the glass and put it to her lips. "Hurry up now, quick, all at once! Let's go . . . the whole thing! No, no! Drink it all. There! That's it," said the large nun. "Now, let's not have any more fuss or I'll call Brother Sean. He has a very convincing friend, a good whacking stick that will help anyone here drink their laxative." With that she turned and left, walking over to the other section of the dormitory.

Sister Barbara continued going to several cots and finally Nilda took a deep breath as she saw the smile on the nun's face directed at her. "You will take this, please. Time for our laxative."

"I already went to the bathroom," said Nilda.

"This is for tomorrow. This way you will be clean and

pure when you greet God. Waking up, you will be ready to release everything in your bowels, getting a fresh start before Mass." Nilda looked and saw that Sister Barbara's smile never left her face. Like it was stuck on or something, she thought. Nilda reached out and took the small glass, holding it up to her lips. A wave of nausea hit her and she closed her eyes. As if anticipating what would happen, the young woman said, "None of that, now. I don't want to call Brother Sean. Nobody here has started this business so don't you be silly. Just drink it down."

Closing her eyes, Nilda began to drink the chalky sticky substance. "All of it, that's a good girl. Go on! Drink it all down. Good. A little bit more. Good. Ah!" Nilda made a heaving sound. "Uh, uh, just swallow and keep it down. Don't let it come up. In a couple of days when you get used to it, you won't even taste it." Smiling, she marched on to the next cot.

Nilda could feel the tears rushing out all at once. Pulling the covers over her head, she began to cry quietly. She licked the tears and welcomed the saltiness as it helped reduce the chalky taste in her mouth. She went on crying quietly until she fell asleep. During the night the sounds of sobbing and whimpering coming from the other cots woke her, but each time she closed her eyes, going back into a deep sleep.

The same large room that was used as the dining room and meeting hall was also used as a classroom. Nilda sat at one of the tables and daydreamed that she was back home. She missed her familiar world of noise, heat, and crowds, and she missed her family most of all. All the nuns, priests, and brothers were very white and had blue or light brown eyes. Only among the children were there dark faces. She wondered if Puerto Ricans were ever allowed to be nuns, fathers, or brothers.

"I hope we can work real hard, children," said the short

nun, "so that when you return home you will be able to receive Holy Communion and make your families happy and proud." She walked around stiffly, stopping to ask the children if they had understood what she had said. She got very little response from anyone.

Papa wouldn't be proud. He would have a fit, thought Nilda, with a feeling of affection and warmth for her stepfather.

That night she looked around at the enormous dormitory with the many rows of army cots set side by side. The chalky taste of the milk of magnesia was still fresh in her mouth, making her feel nauseous.

The lights had been turned out already. She could hear a lot of quiet crying and whimpering. She started to think of home. Why am I here? Did Mama know about this place? She remembered her mother with her portable altars for the Virgin Mary and all the different saints. Nilda's mother set these altars all over the apartment. Always lighting candles, saying prayers, visiting the spiritualist, who gave her all kinds of remedies and special prayers. Mama is always asking God or a saint for miracles. She is always talking about fate and that there is a divine reason for things. "A Destiny. Everything is written for you already up there!" That's what Mama says, she thought. We must not offend God. All of a sudden it all became perfectly clear to Nilda. Wow! I must have done something very bad to offend God! Something really really bad. She started to think about all the "bad" things she had done in her life. After a while she decided that it must be one special thing, or several things, or maybe everything!

Well, whatever it is, I'll repent. I'll repent it all. But now that it was time to repent she realized that she was in bed for the night. Once they put out the lights she could not leave her bunk. She had to do something right now, at that moment. Taking a deep breath, she said, "I promise you, oh Virgin Mary, to sleep all night with my hands folded across

96

my chest just like you look in some of the statues I seen in church. I will recite all the prayers I know and some I just learned. And I promise to think only pure thoughts all night long." Shutting her eyes tightly and folding her arms, she said, "Please, oh please, let me go home tomorrow."

After breakfast the next day, there was a rumor that everyone was going to be sent home. As she heard the children talking, Nilda was both happy and frightened at the same time. Everyone was whispering and talking about going home. In the early afternoon all the campers were called in, assembled in the big dining hall, and seated at the long tables. The large nun entered, walked over to the other nuns, and began whispering. Nilda heard the kids.

"We're gonna be sent home."

"Yeah, that's what I heard."

"Do you think it's true?"

"Maybe. I overheard some of the brothers and they said . . ."

Nilda was afraid to comment or respond lest she break the magic of the miracle that was about to happen. If they knew, it might spoil it all, she thought.

The large nun walked to the front of the hall and began speaking. "I am here for Father Shaw. He had to attend to some urgent business regarding the camp." Nilda's heart was pounding and she could hardly hear or understand what the large woman was saying. "Something has gone wrong with the plumbing and there is no water. Some of you will be sent home today and others will be sent home tomorrow." A huge cheer went up. The children were elated, jumping up and down on the benches. "Stop it! Stop the nonsense or I'll send for Brother Sean this minute," she said, clapping furiously. "Unfortunately," she continued, "we cannot fix the plumbing or the pipes. There is no water available. This is a major repair job which we cannot do this year." This brought giggles and happy sighs from some of the tables. "Quiet, quiet!" she clapped. "Now next year . . ."

Closing her eyes with a sense of joy and relief that shook her body, Nilda stopped listening.

Back in her dormitory, packing away her things in her suitcase, Nilda was filled with happiness at her liberation and secretly guarded her miracle. "It worked!" she whispered. See, she said to herself, just like Mama always says, faith is very powerful! Looking about her and making sure nobody saw her, she made the sign of the cross and whispered, "I'll never doubt You again. I'll be a believer, dear Jesus and Virgin Mary." And so she made her solemn vow right there in the large dormitory, with the very best of intentions.

Niña

by Margarita Mondrus Engle

My mother was afraid it might be our last chance to visit her family in Cuba. The revolution was almost two years old, and already there was talk of an impending crisis.

At the airport in Miami she gave us three instructions.

"Never tell anyone you are tomboys."

"Why?"

"They wouldn't understand. Also, don't tell the other children about your allowance. You have more money in the bank than their fathers make in a year."

"So?"

"So, they would feel bad."

"Oh."

"And the most important, don't bring animals into your grandmother's house."

"But mom . . ."

"No animals. They don't like having animals in the house. Do you understand?"

At the airport in Havana we released the caterpillars we had hidden in our luggage.

"Just in case there are no butterflies here," my sister and I reassured each other.

We had no idea what to expect, but the island did not disappoint us. Abuelita's house was on the outer fringe of Havana, and there were animals everywhere. We put the lizards in beds, and tarantulas and scorpions in the living room. The fisherman who lived across the street gave us a ripe swordfish snout to play with. When it really started to stink my mother threw it on the roof, where it rotted quickly in the sun.

The fisherman's daughter asked me if I had money for ice cream. "Yes," I said with pride, "I have eighty dollars in the bank, which I saved all by myself."

"Dollars? Really?" I could see she didn't believe a word of it. I squirmed inside, remembering my mother's admonition.

"Well, I have something better," the girl offered. "Crabs. When my father gets home you can have one to cook for dinner."

She was right, of course. The crabs were better than my money. Her father came home with a truckload of them, bright orange crabs as big as cats. We put ours on a leash, and led it up and down the street until it died.

My sister liked dogs better than crabs. She begged my mother for a can of dogfood for my great-grandmother's mangy hound. We had to go all the way downtown, to Woolworth's, just to find dogfood in cans. It cost more than a month's supply of real food, corn meal, black beans and rice.

Just to make sure there were no sins left uncommitted, I went across the street and told the fisherman's daughter I was a tomboy.

"Oh no," she said horrified. "You're not a tomboy, don't worry. You will be fine." She fluffed her petticoat and curled a lock of hair with her fingers.

My collection of revolutionary bullets were growing. They were everywhere, in Abuelita's front yard, and in the weeds where we searched for tarantulas, which we caught with wads of gum attached to strings. There were bullets in the open field beyond the city, and in the passion vines which clung to the walls of houses.

On one of my solitary expeditions I wandered far beyond those walls, beyond the open fields and into a mud floored hut with a thatched roof and many inhabitants. The family greeted me as if I had some right to invade their home. The children came outside to introduce me to their mule, their chickens, and the sensitive Mimosa plant which closed its leaves at the touch of a child's finger.

One of the children was called Niña, meaning "girl." I assumed her parents had simply run out of names by the time they got round to her. In Niña's case her name was more unusual than her appearance. She was hardly there, just bones and eyes, and a few pale wisps of hair bleached by malnutrition.

"Doesn't she get enough to eat?" I asked my mother when I reached home.

"They say she has a hole in her stomach."

One day I was standing in the sun of the front porch, watching a black storm cloud sweep across the sky, bringing towards me its thunder and lightning, which fell only in one small corner of the sky. A motionless circle of vultures hung from the cloud, listless, with black wings barely trembling in the wind.

"Come in," my mother warned. "Don't forget your uncle who was killed by lightning, right in his own kitchen."

I ignored her. If it could happen in the kitchen, then why bother to go inside? I was just as safe outside.

Niña crept up to the porch, smiling her death's head smile, like the skull and crossbones on a bottle of medicine.

"Here," she said, offering me half of the anon fruit she was eating. I took it. Together we ate and stared and smiled at each other, not knowing what to say. We both knew my half of the seedy, juicy fruit was going into my body, making flesh and fat, while hers was going right out of the gaping invisible hole in her stomach.

Something like a shiver passed through my shoulder.

"Someone stepped on your grave," Niña giggled.

"What do you mean?"

"They say when you shiver like that it's because someone stepped on the spot where your grave will be."

I stared at Niña's huge eyes, wondering who could have been cruel enough to inform her that she would ever have a grave.

When we trooped down the street to the bingo games at my great-grandmother's house, Niña tagged along. An endless array of uncles and cousins filed in and out, a few boasting revolutionary beards and uniforms, but most outfitted in their farmers' Sunday best, their hands brown and calloused.

Niña was quiet. She poured burnt-milk candy through the hole in her stomach, and watched. The size of her eyes made her watching feel like staring, but no one seemed to notice. Children like Niña surprised no one.

On the anniversary of the revolution the streets filled with truckloads of bearded men on their way to the mountains to celebrate. A man with a loudspeaker walked along our street announcing the treachery of the Yanquis. I was listening inside my grandmother's house. Suddenly his voice changed.

"Let me clarify," he was saying, "that it is not the common people of the United States who we oppose, but the government which has . . ." I stopped listening. Niña was at the open door, smiling her bony smile.

"I told him," she said very quietly, "that you are from Estados Unidos. I didn't want him to hurt your feelings."

At the beach, my sister and I went swimming inside shark fences. We imagined the gliding fins beyond the fence. Afterwards, our mother extracted the spines of bristly sea urchins from the soles of our feet.

We visited huge caverns gleaming with stalactites. How wonderfully the Cuban Indians must have lived, I thought, with no home but a cave, nothing to eat but fruit and shellfish, nothing to do but swim and sing. "We were born a thousand years too late," I told my sister.

With a square old-fashioned camera, I took pictures of pigs, dogs, turkeys, horses and mules. Not once did it occur to me to put a friend or relative into one of my photos. I was from Los Angeles. There were more than enough people in my world, and far too few creatures. When my uncle cut sugar cane, it was the stiff, sweet cane itself which caught my eye, and the gnats clinging to his eyes. His strong arms and wizened face were just part of the landscape. When my cousins picked mamonsillo fruit, it was the tree I looked at, and not the boys showing off by climbing it. I thrived on the wet smell of green land after a rain, and the treasures I found crawling in red mud or dangling from the leaves of weeds and vines. I trapped lizards, netted butterflies, and once, with the help of my sister, I snared a vulture with an elaborate hand-rigged snare. Our relatives were horrified. What could one do with a vulture? It was just the way I felt about everything which mattered to them. If the goal of the revolution was to uproot happy people from their thatched havens, and deposit them in concrete high-rise apartment buildings, who needed it? Thatched huts, after all, were natural, wild, primitive. They were as good as camping. When my mother explained that the people living in the bohios were tired of it, I grew sulky. Only an adult would be foolish enough to believe that any normal human being could prefer comfort to wilderness, roses to weeds, radios to the chants of night-singing frogs.

I knew the hole in Niña's stomach was growing. She was disappearing, vanishing before my eyes. Her parents seemed resigned to her departure. People spoke of her as if she had never really been there. Niña was not solid. She didn't really exist.

On the day of her death, it occurred to me to ask my mother, "Why didn't they just take her to a doctor?"

"They had no money."

I went out to the front porch, abandoning the tarantula I had been about to feed. As I gazed across the open fields toward Niña's bohio, the reality of her death permeated the humid summer air. In my mind, I sifted through a stack of foals and ducks, caterpillars and vultures. Somewhere in that stack, I realized, there should have been an image of Niña.

CHAPTER 5

GROWING UP

A Day in the Life of Me: September 29, 1988

by Leslie Rivera

Hello there! It's me, in real life, as Leslie Rivera. And what an awful life I lead. I have too many sisters, too many brothers and not too much time to lead my own life. Each day seems worse than the others. And every new day that comes, I always ask myself, "What happened to yesterday? Where did it all go?"

Life is a big mystery. No one has the answers, no one has the clues. No one knows why we're stuck in this world of nuclear weapons, homeless people, or people who want more control than anyone else.

Everyone says this is supposed to be the best time of my life, to enjoy it. Well, I have news for them, it's the worst time of my life. I'm sure many others think the same way I do. My old social studies teacher used to say, "They only say that because they're jealous. They never had the freedom kids have now, and they would like to be young again."

I live in a protective environment. Everyone knows me as the "Super's Daughter." Strangers don't talk to me because they all find out about my father. Once this guy told another guy, in Spanish, not to look or talk to me: "She's that super's daughter."

Everyone is always telling me what is good for me and what is not. Me — being a whole thirteen years old — I think I can decide what is good for me and what is not. No one wants to know what the real me is like. They just want to see themselves in other people.

I'm the kind of person that would let other people say their piece and then tell them how right or wrong they are. If they don't like who I am or what I stand for, that is their problem. I stand for myself. They can say whatever they want to about me, but it can never change who I am and what I want to do with my life!

I Love Him Anyway

by Leslie Rivera

They tell me don't bother.
But I don't listen.
I love him anyway.
They tell me not to ask for him.
But I don't listen.
I love him anyway.
I love him.
He's helped me, led me through the rough times.
Always trying to make me laugh,
forget my troubles and fears.
And it works.
He lets my dreams and my hopes
seem possible.
He tells me to make them a reality.
And most of all
I love him simply because
he loves me and is not afraid to show it.
We are joined by something that is
ever so special.
So I am writing this to him,
to let him know no matter where he is,
I'll always be there to tell him,
I love him.

Together

by Leslie Rivera

We walked together on the same path.
We walked as one.
But all of a sudden.
He, who is so special to me,
breaks away.
He makes his own path.
I want to walk with him,
But I am too young,
And the others won't let me.
I stare at him,
till he disappears from my sight.
I stand where he once stood,
and I sob.
We were once together,
But he must go.
I can't tie him down any longer.
He is much too old.
"I must learn to fly alone," he told me.
And now,
when I think of him,
I tell myself,
"He must fly alone,
and I must set him free."

109

HISPANIC, FEMALE AND YOUNG

from Silent Dancing

FIRST LOVE
by Judith Ortiz Cofer

At fourteen and for a few years after, my concerns were mainly focused on the alarms going off in my body warning me of pain or pleasure ahead.

I fell in love, or my hormones awakened from their long slumber in my body, and suddenly the goal of my days was focused on one thing: to catch a glimpse of my secret love. And it had to remain secret, because I had, of course, in the great tradition of tragic romance, chosen to love a boy who was totally out of my reach. He was not Puerto Rican; he was Italian and rich. He was also an older man. He was a senior at the high school when I came in as a freshman. I first saw him in the hall, leaning casually on a wall that was the border line between girlside and boyside for underclassmen. He looked extraordinarily like a young Marlon Brando—down to the ironic little smile. The total of what I knew about the boy who starred in every one of my awkward fantasies was this: that he was the nephew of the man who owned the supermarket on my block; that he often had parties at his parents' beautiful home in the suburbs which I would hear about; that this family had money (which came to our school in many ways)—and this fact made my knees weak: and that he worked at the store near my apartment building on weekends and in the summer.

My mother could not understand why I became so eager to be the one sent out on her endless errands. I pounced on every opportunity from Friday to late Saturday afternoon to go after eggs, cigarettes, milk (I tried to drink as much of it as possible, although I hated the stuff)—the staple items that she would order from the "American" store.

110

Week after week I wandered up and down the aisles, taking furtive glances at the stock room in the back, breathlessly hoping to see my prince. Not that I had a plan. I felt like a pilgrim waiting for a glimpse of Mecca. I did not expect him to notice me. It was sweet agony.

One day I did see him. Dressed in a white outfit like a surgeon; white pants and shirt, white cap, and (gross sight, but not to my love-glazed eyes) blood-smeared butcher's apron. He was helping to drag a side of beef into the freezer storage area of the store. I must have stood there like an idiot, because I remember that he did see me, he even spoke to me! I could have died. I think he said, "Excuse me," and smiled vaguely in my direction.

After that, I willed occasions to go to the supermarket. I watched my mother's pack of cigarettes empty ever so slowly. I wanted her to smoke them fast. I drank milk and forced it on my brother (although a second glass for him had to be bought with my share of Fig Newton cookies which we both liked, but we were restricted to one row each). I gave my cookies up for love, and watched my mother smoke her L&M's with so little enthusiasm that I thought (God, no!) that she might be cutting down on her smoking or maybe even giving up the habit. At this crucial time!

I thought I had kept my lonely romance a secret. Often I cried hot tears on my pillow for the things that kept us apart. In my mind there was no doubt that he would never notice me (and that is why I felt free to stare at him—I was invisible). He could not see me because I was a skinny Puerto Rican girl, a freshman who did not belong to any group he associated with.

At the end of the year I found out that I had not been invisible. I learned one little lesson about human nature—adulation leaves a scent, one that we are all equipped to recognize, and no matter how insignificant the source, we seek it.

In June the nuns at our school would always arrange for

some cultural extravaganza. In my freshman year it was a Roman banquet. We had been studying Greek drama (as a prelude to church history—it was at a fast clip that we galloped through Sophocles and Euripides toward the early Christian martyrs), and our young, energetic Sister Agnes was in the mood for spectacle. She ordered the entire student body (it was a small group of under 300 students) to have our mothers make us togas out of sheets. She handed out a pattern on mimeo pages fresh out of the machine. I remember the intense smell of the alcohol on the sheets of paper, and how almost everyone in the auditorium brought theirs to their noses and inhaled deeply—mimeographed handouts were the school-day buzz that the new Xerox generation of kids is missing out on. Then, as the last couple of weeks of school dragged on, the city of Paterson becoming a concrete oven, and us wilting in our uncomfortable uniforms, we labored like frantic Roman slaves to build a splendid banquet hall in our small auditorium. Sister Agnes wanted a raised dais where the host and hostess would be regally enthroned.

She had already chosen our Senator and Lady from among our ranks. The Lady was to be a beautiful new student named Sophia, a recent Polish immigrant, whose English was still practically unintelligible, but whose features, classically perfect without a trace of makeup, enthralled us. Everyone talked about her gold hair cascading past her waist, and her voice which could carry a note right up to heaven in choir. The nuns wanted her for God. They kept saying that she had a vocation. We just looked at her in awe, and the boys seemed afraid of her. She just smiled and did as she was told. I don't know what she thought of it all. The main privilege of beauty is that others will do almost everything for you, including thinking.

Her partner was to be our best basketball player, a tall, red-haired senior whose family sent its many offsprings to our school. Together, Sophia and her senator looked like the best combination of immigrant genes our community could produce. It did not occur to me to ask then whether anything but their physical beauty qualified them for the starring roles in our production. I had the highest average in the church history class, but I was given the part of one of many "Roman Citizens." I was to sit in front of the plastic fruit and recite a greeting in Latin along with the rest of the school when our hosts came into the hall and took their places on their throne.

On the night of our banquet, my father escorted me in my toga to the door of our school. I felt foolish in my awkwardly draped sheet (blouse and skirt required underneath). My mother had no great skill as a seamstress. The best she could do was hem a skirt or a pair of pants. That night I would have traded her for a peasant woman with a golden needle. I saw other Roman ladies emerging from their parents' cars looking authentic in sheets of material that folded over their bodies like the garments on a statue by Michelangelo. How did they do it? How was it that I always got it just slightly wrong, and worse, I believed that other people were just too polite to mention it. "The poor little Puerto Rican girl," I could hear them thinking. But in reality, I must have been my worst critic, self-conscious as I was.

Soon, we were all sitting at our circle of tables joined together around the dais. Sophia glittered like a golden statue. Her smile was beatific: a perfect, silent Roman lady. Her "senator" looked uncomfortable, glancing around at his buddies, perhaps waiting for the ridicule that he would surely get in the locker room later. The nuns in their black habits stood in the background watching us. What were they supposed to be, the Fates? Nubian slaves? The dancing girls did their modest little dance to tinny music from their finger cymbals, then the speeches were made. Then the grape vine "wine" was raised in a toast to the Roman

Empire we all knew would fall within the week—before finals anyway.

All during the program I had been in a state of controlled hysteria. My secret love sat across the room from me looking supremely bored. I watched his every move, taking him in gluttonously. I relished the shadow of his eyelashes on his ruddy cheeks, his pouty lips smirking sarcastically at the ridiculous sight of our little play. Once he slumped down on his chair, and our sergeant-at-arms nun came over and tapped him sharply on his shoulder. He drew himself up slowly, with disdain. I loved his rebellious spirit. I believed myself still invisible to him in my "nothing" status as I looked upon my beloved. But towards the end of the evening, as we stood chanting our farewells in Latin, he looked straight across the room and into my eyes! How did I survive the killing power of those dark pupils? I trembled in a new way. I was not cold—I was burning! Yet I shook from the inside out, feeling light-headed, dizzy.

The room began to empty and I headed for the girls' lavatory. I wanted to relish the miracle in silence. I did not think for a minute that anything more would follow. I was satisfied with the enormous favor of a look from my beloved. I took my time, knowing that my father would be waiting outside for me, impatient, perhaps glowing in the dark in his phosphorescent white Navy uniform. The others would ride home. I would walk home with my father, both of us in costume. I wanted as few witnesses as possible. When I could no longer hear the crowds in the hallway, I emerged from the bathroom, still under the spell of those mesmerizing eyes.

The lights had been turned off in the hallway and all I could see was the lighted stairwell, at the bottom of which a nun would be stationed. My father would be waiting just outside. I nearly screamed when I felt someone grab me by the waist. But my mouth was quickly covered by someone

114

else's mouth. I was being kissed. My first kiss and I could not even tell who it was. I pulled away to see that face not two inches away from mine. It was he. He smiled down at me. Did I have a silly expression on my face? My glasses felt crooked on my nose. I was unable to move or to speak. More gently, he lifted my chin and touched his lips to mine. This time I did not forget to enjoy it. Then, like the phantom lover that he was, he walked away into the darkened corridor and disappeared.

I don't know how long I stood there. My body was changing right there in the hallway of a Catholic school. My cells were tuning up like musicians in an orchestra, and my heart was a chorus. It was an opera I was composing, and I wanted to stand very still and just listen. But, of course, I heard my father's voice talking to the nun. I was in trouble if he had had to ask about me. I hurried down the stairs making up a story on the way about feeling sick. That would explain my flushed face and it would buy me a little privacy when I got home.

The next day Father announced at the breakfast table that he was leaving on a six month tour of Europe with the Navy in a few weeks and, that at the end of the school year my mother, my brother, and I would be sent to Puerto Rico to stay for half a year at Mama's (my mother's mother) house. I was devastated. This was the usual routine for us. We had always gone to Mama's to stay when Father was away for long periods. But this year it was different for me. I was in love, and . . . my heart knocked against my bony chest at this thought . . . he loved me too? I broke into sobs and left the table.

In the next week I discovered the inexorable truth about parents. They can actually carry on with their plans right through tears, threats, and the awful spectacle of a teenager's broken heart. My father left me to my mother who impassively packed while I explained over and over that I was at a crucial time in my studies and that if I left my entire life would be ruined. All she would say is, "You are an intelligent girl, you'll catch up." Her head was filled with visions of casa and family reunions, long gossip sessions with her mama and sisters. What did she care that I was losing my one chance at true love?

In the meantime I tried desperately to see him. I thought he would look for me too. But the few times I saw him in the hallway, he was always rushing away. It would be long weeks of confusion and pain before I realized that the kiss was nothing but a little trophy for his ego. He had no interest in me other than as his adorer. He was flattered by my silent worship of him, and he had bestowed a kiss on me to please himself, and to fan the flames. I learned a lesson about the battle of the sexes then that I have never forgotten: the object is not always to win, but most times simply to keep your opponent (synonymous at times with "the loved one") guessing.

But this is too cynical a view to sustain in the face of that overwhelming rush of emotion that is first love. And in thinking back about my own experience with it, I can be objective only to the point where I recall how sweet the anguish was, how caught up in the moment I felt, and how every nerve in my body was involved in this salute to life. Later, much later, after what seemed like an eternity of dragging the weight of unrequited love around with me, I learned to make myself visible and to relish the little battles required to win the greatest prize of all. And much later, I read and understood Camus' statement about the subject that concerns both adolescent and philosopher alike: if love were easy, life would be too simple.

Teenage Zombie

by Amina Susan Ali

My younger sister, Millie, had curly black hair that she refused to cut for as long as we lived with our mother in a railroad apartment on Ludlow Street. We grew up in the kitchen, in front of the stove cooking rice and beans and Spam, at the window hanging up and taking down laundry, and around the kitchen table with various visitors and relatives on summer nights, sucking on ice cubes because there was never enough money to buy soda for everyone.

Millie looked a lot like me—she had the same eyes and the same smile—but she was darker. She was also darker than Mami and Papi. When Mami lost her temper she called Millie a nigger. Millie set her hair on empty soda cans to make it look straight. When it rained, she wouldn't go out if she could help it, and she rarely went swimming.

When we were home alone we'd put the radio on full blast and dance on the furniture. The best spot was on top of the couch because you could see yourself in the big mirror on the living room wall. One time we gave a show and invited the kids from the neighborhood. For an opening act, Miguel from next door did a magic act. He showed the audience a baseball card and said he was going to make it disappear. Then he told everyone to close their eyes, but everybody started booing him. Carmen threw her M&M's at him and then some of the other kids started throwing popcorn up in the air, so we had to make him stop. He was five years old.

Then Millie and I came on. I had tied celery and lettuce leaves in my hair and wore a white sheet wrapped around me and tied around my waist and across my chest with a piece of rope, like someone from ancient Greece. Millie wore my pink ballet leotard and a lace curtain around her shoulders. We danced to a Tito Rodríguez record. It was too bad the record player kept stopping and starting, but everybody liked it anyway.

When Millie turned thirteen she started going to a little church two blocks from our house. From the outside it just looked like a metal door, so I had passed it many times without noticing it. Soon Millie stopped smoking and playing hooky. She stayed away from the kids on the block, no longer stopping to listen to rock & roll on the transistor radios on weekend nights. Though we were all baptized Catholics Mami didn't object to Millie's new interest. In fact, she seemed relieved that Millie wasn't heading in the direction of the other girls in the neighborhood.

One Sunday Frankie, one of the guys from the block, and I were sitting in Washington Square Park. It was summer, it was 1967 and I was sixteen. We were sitting on a bench near the chess players, when this guy came over and sat next to us, not too close, but close enough, and started reading this book, *Catcher in the Rye*. Nobody said anything for a long time, then all of a sudden Frankie said, "Why are you so quiet, Angie?" Then the guy who was sitting next to us put the book down and said, "That's not what you should say!" Then he got down on his *knees*, right in front of me, and said, "Spill your guts to me and I'm yours forever."

I just looked at him. I guess I didn't know what to say. He stood up and said, "O.K., I guess that doesn't work either." He stuck out his hand. "Hi. My name's Jim." Frankie and I introduced ourselves and he started talking to us just like somebody off the block. It turned out that he was living a few blocks from us. The three of us spent the rest of the day together. I was surprised that he didn't feel uncomfortable, not knowing whether or not Frankie was my boyfriend. But Jim didn't think that way. He had run away from Michigan and thought New York was a great place. As it turned out, he had seen more of the city that summer than I had seen in my whole life.

118

The reason Frankie and I were in the park talking that day was that Frankie had wanted to go out with Millie. Millie knew this but because Frank was Black she didn't want anything to do with him. I remember the afternoon she came home and told me that Frankie liked her. She was furious. She kept repeating, "Is he color blind? Doesn't he have eyes?" I felt like asking her, "Do you?" because she was almost as dark as he was. But because we were Puerto Rican, she didn't think so. I was trying to explain this to Frankie without hurting his feelings.

As I said before, Millie had started going to this church. She brought Mami to church with her, then she brought me. It was a pretty nice church. They had an organ, two guitars, a guy who played saxophone, a drummer, and a lot of the sisters played tambourines. All the services were held in Spanish. We started going on Sunday mornings, then to the Young People's meetings on Wednesday nights, but the best meetings were on Sunday nights. Everybody came to church then, even the little kids and babies. Piles of diapers were laid in the aisles and formula and juice bottles rested on the floor inside the pews. I liked to watch the minister walk up and down the platform, up and down, up and down, back and forth, then all of a sudden he'd jump, then he'd be walking back and forth again, constantly preaching, then he'd start talking a little faster and a little louder, then he'd repeat something over and over again, then bang his Bible on the pulpit, and somebody would yell Hallelujah and somebody else would yell something else and then practically the whole church would be yelling and shouting and carrying on, then after a little while they'd quiet down, and the minister would pick up where he left off and go right on preaching. They'd carry on like that for hours.

I liked the church and kept going to services. Once, a group of us from the Young People's Society visited an English speaking church. Their service was a lot quieter than ours. Millie seemed to like it there. They had clean white pews and a red carpet, instead of tired brown wood pews and floors and old pictures of Jesus like our church. Soon after Millie started making excuses as to why she didn't want to go to the Spanish church. She said her Spanish wasn't that good and she couldn't understand much of what was going on. My Spanish wasn't so good either but I had both an English and Spanish bible, and every night I'd read something from the Spanish bible, then re-read the parts I didn't understand in English. I told Millie that she should have done the same but she didn't seem to want to try. She said she had enough trouble reading English.

After a while she started going to the English-speaking church by herself regularly, and eventually joined. Then I noticed that she got annoyed every time I spoke to her in Spanish. She'd ask, "Can't you speak English? What's wrong with you?" Pretty soon after she would only associate with her friends from the American church, as if they were more holy than anyone else.

A couple of months later, she was preparing for the SATs. She mentioned that some of the girls in her class told her that they could guess on the vocabulary because they knew Spanish. And then Millie, my sister, said, "But that doesn't help me because I'm not Spanish." Not I can't *speak* Spanish, but I'm not Spanish. So I said, "What are you, then, Millie?" She said, "I'm American." So I said, "Yeah, sure, you're Puerto Rican." She said there was no such thing. Puerto Rico wasn't a country, so how could anybody be Puerto Rican? I said I didn't know anything about all that, all I knew was that there was something called American and I was not it. She said that was the wrong way to think and that God made us all the same. I said, if we're all the same, why did the Americans have white pews and a red carpet in their church while we had broken-down wood pews and old floors? She said she didn't know what I was talking about, she didn't care what her church looked like, and that there was no such thing as Puerto Rican, she was not one, and she did not speak Spanish.

I was also trying to explain all this to Frankie that Sunday afternoon, but soon lost my ambitions after meeting Jim.

Jim and I got to be really good friends. He was eighteen years old and read a lot. He had sandy colored hair and was the first American who spoke to me with some purpose other than to tell me what to do. He listened to what I said instead of putting his eyes on me and his ears someplace else. He wore sneakers all the time and carried paperback books and newspapers wherever he went. He wore T-shirts and jeans and his hair was always dripping into his face.

I knew I really liked him, but he wasn't of the faith, he was of the world. I wasn't supposed to have a boyfriend who wasn't a Christian. And as far as my mother was concerned, I wasn't supposed to have a boyfriend, period. Boys only got girls in trouble, she had taught us, the proof being the other girls in the neighborhood who all had babies by the time they were sixteen. And then there were the stories about our father, how he was like every other man who couldn't be counted on. It seemed the only men who could ever meet with her approval were somewhere far away or very rich.

Every night that summer we'd meet in front of his building except for Sundays, and Wednesdays, when I went to church. We'd go for a walk, or go get pizza, or go to the park. I couldn't bring him home because of my mother, and I had to be indoors by 9:30 because she got home from the restaurant where she worked at a quarter to ten, so that put a limit on the amount of time we spent together. Sometimes we'd hold hands or else he'd put his arm around me, which started getting me worried about meeting somebody from church in the street, so I would manage to find an excuse, like complaining about the heat, to put a quick end to *that*.

One night we didn't have any money between us and

really didn't know what to do. It was about ninety degrees and I was bored and angry because I had been in the house all day and ended up having an argument with my mother over doing the ironing. When I met Jim outside he suggested that we go to his house, and I agreed. I felt I had stepped into a foreign country. The apartment was filled with psychedelic posters, rock albums, and furniture I had seen in the street. What would my mother think, I thought, what would the people at church think if they knew I had a friend like this?

I sat at the kitchen table, my usual post at home. Jim said a few things to me and I answered, not hearing what I was saying, but feeling the sounds in my head. He put his arms on my shoulders, bent over and kissed my face a few times. I closed my eyes—I wanted to so much—then quickly opened them looking at the floor and just managing to say, "No, I can't, that's all." I heard him half-laugh, half-gasp, like, this was one of my jokes, right? So he said, "Come on, Angie, we're only human, God will understand," trying to make a joke out of it.

I stood up and ran out of the apartment, down the dark stairs and into the night. When I got home Millie was there, folding laundry and singing to herself in an expressionless voice. She wore a white slip and had her hair set on soda cans.

"Where were you?" she asked. "I thought you'd be home for dinner. Did you eat?"

"No, I'm not very hungry. I went someplace with a friend and got lost on my way home."

It was too hot to try to make sense out of everything, so I started to get ready for bed. I never spoke to Jim again.

Memories of Her

by Amina Susan Ali

In the photograph she is younger and darker than I remember her. She is smiling and leaning against a palm tree, wearing a two-piece bathing suit with a scarf tied around her head. That was before I knew her. When I knew her she wore dresses, teased hair and red lipstick.

She was always complaining because I was "fresh." I couldn't understand why fresh meant bad. The milk was fresh and that meant it was good, but my being fresh meant a smack on the mouth. She used to tell me I was supposed to obey and if I didn't want to I had something evil in me, and if it got too evil she was going to have to take me to a place where they would pour holy water on me and burn incense.

The thought of her admitting how bad I was to another person embarrassed me so much that I would be quiet for a day or two, eat everything she fed me, even broccoli, wouldn't scream when she didn't have enough coffee to pour a little into my Donald Duck cup, and above all, I would never ask, "Where's Daddy?"

When we were around other people I was supposed to smile and act right. "Acting Right" meant not talking too much but not being too quiet either, not spilling or breaking anything, and for God's sake, not being or getting dirty. I never seemed to strike the right balance with her because afterwards she would say I had hurt her feelings because I hadn't wanted to talk to her friend, aunt, sister-in-law or cousin, or because I had said the wrong thing, or because I had asked a question about something that wasn't supposed to exist. Soon I learned to endure these visits by asking to turn on the T.V. and then falling asleep in front of it.

She taught me at a very early age the rules of behavior I would have to follow if I wanted to survive in the real world.

Rule Number One: Don't expect too much. "Too much" meant what you wanted. Too much meant the sky. That's why I wasn't allowed on the roof. But on days when she was at work and I was on hooky leave, I would open the Frankenstein door, shudder at the loud scraping noise it made and, after waiting a few seconds to see if anyone was coming, sit on the tar and look up at that blue that went on endlessly, that sea. The first time I went to the beach I remember running up to her to shake her hand, because she, unlike anyone else I knew personally, had been to Europe and back.

I'd look up from the tired, slumping roof at the sparrows circling around and around, and my eyes would follow the one or two that would fly in the opposite direction, or just go off on their own way. Those were the ones that made me lose faith in the desirability of being human over other forms of life.

Human life, as far as I could see, sure was a drag. It was being proper and acting right and not having too much to tell in Confession. But no matter what I did or did not do, or say or did not say, there was always something that I was doing or saying wrong. I couldn't go to science camp when a teacher urged me to because that would encourage my nasty habit of collecting bugs, rocks, and reptiles. Why didn't I prefer the companionship of pink plastic rollers, Simplicity patterns and pots and pans? Why did I hang out in the park all alone till it was almost dark, and sometimes even when it was already dark? What was I doing there? Did I expect anyone to believe that I was just watching the trees and the lake and the questionable things that swam around in it? Why couldn't I be like Carmen, who tweezed her eyebrows, shaved her legs and won twist contests at age ten?

But I couldn't care less about Carmen. Or her kind. I was totally embroiled in my first and only love, Joan of Arc. I learned all about Joan of Arc on TV in a movie they showed one day when I was playing hooky from junior high school. With that short hair and armor, jumping on her horse, leading her troops to battle—I knew this was for me. It sure beat being a secretary or waitress, and the Catholic Church even made her a saint. But who was I going to lead, and for what cause? There weren't any wars going on, at least not in my neighborhood, and I wasn't allowed to go on the West Side. Nonetheless, I cut my own hair, slept on the floor because I heard that's how saints had visions, and waited for my voices. In the meantime, I practiced being misunderstood.

My home became the perfect training ground for martyrdom. Contrary to popular belief, the Spanish Inquisition commenced the first time a Puerto Rican girl came home five minutes late. It was torture first, questioning later. Confessions were meaningless because no matter what you said, it didn't mean shit.

"I'm your mother!"—smack! "Don't you forget that."

Did I really have to be reminded.

MONICA

by INEZ SANTANA

"There she goes — that girl, Monica, I was telling you about," Amanda said to Laura.

"Is that the one you said thinks she's black?"

"Yep, that's her." They giggled as Monica walked away.

Monica was used to people saying that she acted black, even though her mother was Puerto Rican and her father was Colombian. But little did these foolish people know how much they could still hurt her inside. At times even she started to think she did act black, but why? Why did people tell her that? Monica really didn't know. Maybe it was because she preferred black boys, or because black boys preferred her over dark-skinned girls, for she was light-skinned, and had long hair.

The same day she was walking to the train station with her close friend Dee-Dee. As they walked down the stairs they could hear some Hispanic boys talking about the girls in their school. When they passed them, the boys kind of quieted down, but as they walked to the back of the train station, Monica heard some guy tell his friend to go up to her. She really was not in the mood to be insulted, so she kept on walking to her destination, which was the back of the train. Then one of the guys from the group of boys approached her.

"Cómo estás?" he asked.

"Excuse me," Monica answered with a puzzled face.

"I'm sorry. I'm just so used to speaking Spanish. I meant to say, how are you doing?" he spoke with a Spanish accent.

"I'm fine, and yourself?"

"I'm okay. My name is Juan, what is yours?"

"My name is Monica." She answered him with a bit of resistance. Just as he was about to say something else, the

126

Number 6 train came. As Monica got on, she thought herself lucky that the train had come just in time.

Juan walked back to his friends in the front of the train. He was in a daze for he finally met the girl he had liked since the beginning of school.

"Yo man, what happened?" his friend Miguel asked him.

"Nada, bro. It's just that I met the girl of my dreams."

"That girl Monica who thinks she's a morena? She's no good — get a girl who knows she's Puertoriqueña."

"Well I like her, and I don't care what you think." But Juan thought to himself that maybe his friend was right.

Meanwhile Monica was in the back of the train talking and just having a good time when the guy she liked — the one who went to the school across the street from hers — walked onto the train with about three of his friends. He didn't notice her at first, but after a while he did and it seemed like he was happy to see her. As Monica was talking to Dee-Dee, she would look his way and just smile trying to get his attention. It seemed like he wanted to get her attention too, but he just didn't know how. Finally, when the train got to 86th Street, one of his friends got the courage to go up to Dee-Dee. After he introduced the rest of his friends, Dee-Dee introduced Monica.

"How you doing, lovely?" the boy said to Monica.

"Fine," Monica answered, thinking to herself, don't these guys have any other way to start a conversation.

"My name is Shawn, what's yours?"

"My name is Monica."

After talking for a little while and getting to know each other better, he asked her if she was black. Monica answered truthfully, and she told him she was 100 percent Hispanic. It took him a while to actually believe her because he said she sounded like a black girl and that she also dressed like a black girl. She didin't know how that was possible — as far as she knew, she was just dressing the way she liked to dress.

Shawn then asked, "Is it possible that me and you can go out one day or at least keep in touch with each other?"

"There is a possibility that we can go out," answered Monica with a bit of a smirk. She took his number just in time, for it was 110th Street and the next stop was hers.

She spent most of the next few weeks with Shawn, going to the movies, taking walks, or just hanging out in front of her building. One day they went for pizza together. There was a crowd of kids in front, but Monica didn't care. She just wanted some pizza. The only problem was that the crowd was Juan and his friends, and as she walked inside the pizzeria, all the guys turned around and looked at her. She wondered why they were all staring at her like that.

"I told you she thinks she's a morena. Look at her walking with that moreno."

"Just because she's walking with a moreno doesn't mean she thinks she's black," Juan said to Miguel defending Monica.

When they were inside the pizzeria, Shawn was very upset. He didn't like the way the guys outside were looking at Monica. Just as he was about to go outside and ask the boys what they were looking at, Monica cut into his thoughts.

"Are you upset?" she asked.

"No, it's just I don't like the way they were looking at you."

"It's nothing. I think that they just don't like the fact that a Puerto Rican girl is walking with a black person, or, for that matter, with anyone of another nationality. Just don't worry about it."

When they walked outside, Juan approached her and said "Hi." Since she hadn't even thought about Juan since she last saw him on the train, she answered, "Hi, what have you been up to lately?"

"Nothing much," answered Juan. And Monica turned and left with Shawn.

The weeks to come were somewhat confusing for Monica. People started to say that she should be with Juan, not with Shawn. She asked her friends for some advice and they told her not to listen to what people said. Her real friends would leave it up to her to see whoever she wanted to see.

One day when Monica was coming home from school, she saw Juan with one of her close friends. She thought to herself what a DOG!! Then she saw Shawn, but as she walked towards him, a girl came out of the school and hugged him. Monica was furious and very hurt — she thought he had really liked her. When Shawn saw her, he just stopped in his tracks and then started towards her, but she walked away and went down the stairs into the train station. When she got on the train, she thought to herself, it doesn't matter what skin color or nationality they are, most boys are the same.

I Thought You Loved Me

by Michelle Calero

Part I

On her way home from school, Carmen decided to stop by the bodega and get something to drink. "What are you going to get, Carmen," asked her friend Dora.

"Maybe a Coke, even though Mami hates it when I drink it. Some sob story about it being bad for you. Big deal. If that was true, every teenager on this earth would be in the hospital. I don't care. One little can of soda never hurt anyone."

The two girls went into the corner grocery store, and they each bought a can of soda. Then Carmen saw him stand there. The new kid on the block who went by the name of Chico. He had just come from Puerto Rico and it showed. Brown skin tone, dark brown hair, deep brown eyes. He was perfect. Perfect in every way. He was smart (they were in the same class), he was extremely good looking, and she knew he was nice, even though the only words he ever spoke to her were, "Excuse me."

Carmen had to talk with him. She just had to. So Carmen told Dora, "Go on ahead, I have to buy something else."

"Don't worry Carmen, I can take a hint." Dora walked out, acting like a true best friend. Carmen walked over to the rack where the snack-sized cakes were and carefully selected something that cost more money than she had in her pocket. When the clerk announced to her, loud enough for Chico to hear, that the cake cost fifty cents, Carmen magnanimously said that she only had forty cents.

"I got it," said Chico, and placed a shiny silver dime on the counter.

"Thank you," she said, and gave him a piece of the cake.

"Don't mention it. So where you headed?"

"Home," she said. She couldn't believe she was actually talking to him.

"And where is your home?"

"About five blocks away, on Mango Street."

"If you want, I can walk you home. I only live two blocks from Mango Street so it's not really out of my way."

Carmen thought she had died and gone to heaven.

"Sure."

The two teenagers began walking, and about five minutes later, Carmen found her hand holding his. She only wished the walk had been longer.

Part II

Monday morning Carmen told Dora what had happened that day at the store. "I'm sorry I couldn't call to tell you sooner, but I had to go shopping with my mother."

"That's okay."

As the girls were walking down the school corridor, they saw Chico heading in their direction. He just passed Carmen by. She was shocked. She couldn't believe that after what happened on Friday he would act cold and not even give her as much as a glance or a hello.

During lunch outside, Carmen tried to get his attention. She called him, "Hi, Chico!"

"What? Oh yeah. Hi, uh, Carmen."

"Thanks again about Friday."

There was no response. When Carmen looked up from examining her sneakers, he was gone. Once again she was shrugged off by Chico. What was going on?

Part III

Carmen called Dora and asked her what she should do about Chico. She knew she could count on Dora to listen and give her the right advice. "I don't know what to do, Dora," she confided. "After what happened in the store and everything, I thought. . . ."

"Carmen, I'm going to tell you something that I think will make you happy." Carmen expected to hear something good about Dora's family. She never expected what she was about to learn. "About a week ago, I asked Chico if he liked you. He said he would tell me at lunch. I don't know what happened, but he never told me."

"Yeah? Go on."

"Well, the next day he came up to me at lunch and he said he did like you. Then I asked him if he wanted me to tell you and he said 'No, that's okay, I'll do it myself.'"

"But then how come he's been ignoring me?"

Part IV

After weeks of constantly being ignored, Carmen soon got tired of running home and crying. No more tears could fall from her eyes. Then she came to a decision. She would confront him, one on one. No friends, no notes. It was now or never. This was just something she had to do.

She planned everything very carefully, what she would say and when she would say it. She decided that the best time was at lunch, where they could walk around and settle things. Between classes was not a good time because too many people would be crowded in the halls, and everyone was usually in a hurry. Yes, lunch was the best time. They would have plenty of time to talk, and the atmosphere would be relaxed.

The next day, after the lunch bell rang, Carmen felt a tightening in her stomach. She ignored it.There was only one week until graduation and again, it was now or never. She waited by the cafeteria door. Chico passed by, and of course, she was brushed off. She quickly ate her lunch and waited until he was done to catch him walking through the door into the yard.

"Chico, come here."

Chico slowly walked up to her and said, "Yeah?"

"Look, there's something I've been wanting to tell you and I . . . ."

"Look, I'm sorry I've been ignoring you. I just had to think things over, and I've made up my mind. Would you go out with me?"

Carmen couldn't believe what she was hearing. She had been waiting for this moment all year.

"I'm sorry, Chico. I only think of you as a friend and nothing more." Chico walked away with a sad look of disappointment on his face.

A Lost Friend

by Ivy Colomba

I really don't understand, so many of my friends from my old school are pregnant. Why? Does it mean you are mature if you become pregnant? To me, it means a person has to stay home and take care of a baby. It also means a person (usually the girl) has to give up part of her social life. Many girls have babies, then their boyfriends desert them, and they are left all alone to bring up their children.

One of my friends who got pregnant comes from a family that doesn't offer exactly the best role models on earth. All of her brothers and sisters have been in jail more than once. Two of her brothers are serving sentences for drug dealing. Her sisters have about three children each, and none of them is over twenty-two. Even her mother has been in jail. My friend was held back twice and she is only in the grade above me even though she is three years older.

She had gotten pregnant by a seventeen year old boy. No one knew it until she went into the hospital . . . she was only five months pregnant when the baby was born. There were so many rumors. Some said her sister had given her a "homemade" abortion which did not work and only made her sick. Another rumor was that she wore a girdle and that forced her baby out.

When she went into the hospital, her mother didn't even want to see her. She said, and I quote, "I disown my daughter." Her boyfriend was in the hospital with her every day. She had tubes coming out of her from everywhere. When blood would trickle down her mouth, her boyfriend was there, and he would always clean it up. The baby was a girl.

Everyone thought she would be okay in a week or two, but they were wrong. My aunt, who was her third and fourth grade teacher in elementary school, called me one afternoon. I picked up the telephone. Her voice sounded as if she had been crying. I asked her what was wrong, and she said that my friend had died. Immediately tears began to roll down my cheeks. I could not believe it, a friend of mine had actually died. Why? For days I would ask myself, why did God take the life of someone so young? Sometimes when I would cry, my uncles would tell me not to, but how could I not cry when she was a friend of mine?

It took time for me to get over her death. Doesn't it always take time? Some people tell me, "How could you ever hang around a girl like her, she could have influenced you to do something like that."

She was my friend — how could anyone say such a thing?

Her boyfriend was supposed to marry her as soon as she got out of the hospital, but he never got the chance. His family is out in Texas, and he is supposed to take the baby with him. I see him a lot around the playground of my old school with his brothers and his friends. When I see him, he is always happy, as if nothing ever happened. It's probably because a person cannot stay sad forever when they lose someone.

I look at my class pictures and see her in them. I can't believe she is dead. Why, it seems like just yesterday we were hanging out in the playground of our old school and laughing. I can't understand it.

The worst thing in the world I can think of is losing a friend.

Caught by Life

by Edna Robles

This is a case of a teenage pregnancy.

Her name is Marisol. She is sixteen, a school dropout since she was thirteen, and made pregnant by a twenty-year-old man. Her family is crazed.

Because of the way she was raised, Marisol is very rowdy. Her parents tried to make the neighbors think that they were concerned about her, but they were not. Marisol knew this, and she was not afraid to admit it.

Marisol got her reputation when she was nine. She was out on the street till two o'clock in the morning. Her parents didn't mind. They only wanted to know where she was, and that was all. No curfew, no nothing. When she was a little older, she would sleep with all the guys she thought were cute or popular (all the more reason).

She used to live with her family in a cramped four-room apartment. Her parents had one room and her brother and his new girl had another room. They moved Marisol into the living room.

Now, at present, Marisol is still the same. She said love really hit her this time. But it hasn't. She is doing the same thing. She still dates guys that aren't worth it.

When she calls me up at times, I can tell that her innocence is shattered. My parents try to keep me from speaking to her. They think our friendship may have some kind of bad effect on me. She doesn't have many friends because of the way she is. Many parents, like mine, stop their children from being friends with her. All of these problems have a very damaging effect on her.

Marisol told me that sometimes she wasn't sure whose baby it was. She was just planning to keep the child "for the hell of it," which meant only to keep a hold on the guy.

She moved in with her boyfriend, which is not great because he makes his money selling drugs. But at least he didn't dump her while she was carrying the baby. This shows you that all guys don't always run away from their responsibilities. At least he faced them. But selling drugs is the wrong way. He should have gotten a decent job so that he could proudly say, "I worked to the bone for my child, and I'm proud of it." But, unfortunately, he will not be able to say that because selling drugs is not working to the bone.

Marisol is doing it all wrong.

Marisol called me yesterday. She told me she quit smoking. She said that her boyfriend helped her stop. She was lying — she just wants people to like him. She also said that he told her to return to school next year. She claims she likes school. I let her borrow some books of mine. She said she is going to study them, but she really doesn't. She only does it to impress me. Marisol does not want people to think of her badly. She doesn't want to have a worse reputation than she already has.

Now you may wonder how can a person make progress with all of this? You better believe it, she did. Her progress has been rather slow. But it's happening, all right. Recently, Marisol gave me a poem that she wrote claiming that she has changed her ways and is involved with only one guy:

> Two people in love,
> not knowing how to face each other.
> Scared to realize
> they are two broken hearts.
> One comes along to say
> how much he means to her,
> and how much she cares.
> A heart that didn't let love pass by.
> But when one denies
> the love from another,
> it just means no.

Time has passed and Marisol has had an abortion. She calls me up and tells me how things are going. I can tell that they are not going very well. She only calls me when she has a problem. But she never comes out with it and says it. She knows I can tell when there is something wrong. She tries to pretend things are fine when they really aren't. She thinks she is pregnant again.

They broke up, and he threw her out of the house. But when she went back to get her things, he wanted her back and she stayed. They are trying to work out a schedule so that she can live with her family and be with him at the same time. I suggested that she stay with her family during the week and stay over at his place during the weekends, but this did not work out because he thought she might go behind his back and cheat on him.

Marisol's life has a connection with Las Mujeres. She is Hispanic, Puerto Rican to be exact. Although she acts as if she were a woman, she really does not know who she is. She is still just a young girl, out there fighting as if she were in a jungle, as if a lion were chasing her, as if life were catching her before her time.

Inequalities

by Nereida Román

Not only in the Hispanic culture but in every culture males and females are treated differently. My family isn't an exception. I have an older brother named Miguel. He is a year and nine months older than me, but my parents treat me as if I were much younger. My parents let Miguel do almost whatever he wants. They tell me, "later when you're older." They have been giving me that same line for over a year. I'm sick of hearing that same line.

I remember once last summer I was going to the store, and my mother wouldn't let me go to the store by myself. She said, "You can't go alone, take Carlos with you." Carlos is my younger brother — at the time he was only eight years old.

A few days later Carlos, my father, and I went to a park. Carlos asked my father if he could go to the store. My father said, "Okay son, need some money?" Later on that same day I asked my father if I could go to the store. He made me take my brother.

I'm sure that I'm not alone. I know a lot of people with the same problem. I seem to be the first to speak out about it. I hope that this story will encourage more girls with the same problem as I have to speak out.

NEVER FITTING IN

by NEREIDA ROMÁN

As you may have guessed, my name is Nereida Román. If you don't think that you can pronounce it, you're not alone. Almost nobody can. It's a strange name to go with a strange person, as you will probably notice when you read what I've written.

I'm thirteen and in the eighth grade. No, I wasn't skipped. I started school early. I think that was one of the dumbest things I ever did. It means I could probably graduate from high school when I'm sixteen.

I'm strange! I've always done things differently. For example, all the girls in school are into boys, music and more boys. I don't like boys. Well, I like them a little, but they're not as important to me as they are to some of the other girls.

I've been the kind of person that never fits in right, but the thing that has bothered me the most is being called a "tomboy." After that comes, of course, being called a "nerd" (which, because of my age and grade, seems to be the truth). And if kids have nothing else to bother me about, they bother me about my hair. It never seems to stay in the right place.

I don't see why people make such a big deal about a girl playing "boys' games." I don't even see why people say that most sports are boys' sports. To me all sports are for everybody. But people never think of it from my point of view. I don't think that there is anything wrong with a girl playing football, basketball or any other sport.

Everybody makes fun of me. "Tomboy, why don't you act like a girl?" they say to me. I don't understand what they want me to act like. Girls don't act a certain way. If I want to play sports, I think that it's my business. Even if other people don't think that it is acceptable, I think they should mind their own business.

I was on the school basketball team. I was the only girl on the team. During the entire season I only got one pass. From the beginning of the season all the way to the end, I was never accepted by any other member of the team. I was really bothered at first. I was so bothered that I quit the team, but I noticed then that when I was on the team, I was having a lot of fun, more than I ever thought. So I joined the team again, but I still don't fit in right. They still bother me to this day, but I don't pay much attention to them anymore.

I'm not too sure why I turned out to be a tomboy, but I think it had something to do with my having lived among boys, five older than me and one younger. I didn't have an older sister or live with any other girls. My mother raised me, my two brothers, and the other four boys as equals. I played almost every sport you can think of when I was younger, and I still do now. I always thought that there was nothing wrong with having fun my way but, of course, nobody agrees with me.

I'm not the only tomboy in my family, but I'm the first. Sometimes I think that some of my cousins have followed my example. I hope they don't have the same problems that I, and probably all the tomboys in the world, have had. I'm not sure if my cousins look up to me, or if they just like sports. I never told them that it's okay to be different, but every now and then, they tell me.

That Something Special: Dancing with the Repertory Dance Company of Harlem

by Leslie Rivera

They tell me
that I have that something special.
But I don't see it the way they do.
That something
is what I give to them
my audience
and what I get back in return
is amazing.
I pour out my heart,
my soul, and every little dream
that I have.
People see it
and respond.
It is the sole reason I dance.
It is my way of reaching out
touching the world
letting it see my dreams and hopes.
It's that something special
that makes me give to my audiences
that makes them know what I feel.
And for them to see that
is an accomplishment all its own.

Origen

by Judith Ortiz Cofer

What we want to know:
in the unimaginable moment
of the union of parental flesh,
was there love, or
are we the heirs of carelessness?
This matters,
That we were wanted; called forth
to fulfill a wish.
That we were meant to be.

Thinking

by Lorna Dee Cervantes

I think I grew up last year.
Or maybe today
is just a phase,
like Autumn's bright red foliage
just before Winter's death.
Sometimes I think that maybe
life
is nothing but
one big phase
waiting for the next,
and death
is what you have
when you run out of phases.
I think that maybe
I did grow up . . .
some.

CHAPTER 6

A LAS MUJERES

Fulana

by Judith Ortiz Cofer

She was the woman with no name. The blank filled in
with Fulana in the presence of children.
But we knew her—she was the wild girl
we were not allowed to play with,
who painted her face with her absent mother's make-up,
and who always wanted to be "wife"
when we played house. She was bored
with other games, preferred to turn the radio loud
to songs about women and men
loving and fighting to guitar, maracas, and drums.
She wanted to be a dancer on the stage,
dressed in nothing but yellow feathers.

And she would grow up careless as a bird,
losing contact with her name during the years
when her body was light enough to fly.
But gravity began to pull her down
to where the land animals chewed the cud
of domestic routine, she was a different
species. She had become Fulana, the creature
bearing the jagged scars of wings on her back,
whose name should not be mentioned
in the presence of impressionable little girls
who might begin to wonder about flight,
how the houses of their earth-bound mothers,
the fields and rivers, and the schools and churches
would look from above.

from Silent Dancing

VidA

by JudiTH OrTiz CofER

To a child, life is a play directed by parents, teachers, and other adults who are forever giving directions: "Say this," "Don't say that," "Stand here," "Walk this way," "Wear these clothes," and on and on and on. If we miss or ignore a cue, we are punished. And so we memorized the script of our lives as interpreted by our progenitors, and we learned not to extemporize too much: the world—our audience—likes the well-made play, with everyone in their places and not too many bursts of brilliance or surprises. But once in a while new characters walk onto the stage, and the writers have to scramble to fit them in, and for a while, life gets interesting.

Vida was a beautiful Chilean girl who simply appeared in the apartment upstairs with her refugee family one day and introduced herself into our daily drama.

She was tall, thin and graceful as a ballerina, with fair skin and short black hair. She looked like a gazelle as she bounded down the stairs from her apartment to ours the day she first came to our door to borrow something. Her accent charmed us. She said that she had just arrived from Chile with her sister, her sister's newborn baby girl, her sister's husband, and their grandmother. They were all living together in a one-bedroom apartment on the floor above us.

There must have been an interesting story of political exile there, but I was too young to care about that detail. I was immediately fascinated by the lovely Vida who looked like one of the models in the fashion magazines that I, just turning twelve, had begun to be interested in. Vida came into my life during one of my father's long absences with the Navy, so that his constant vigilance was not a hindrance to my developing attachment to this vibrant human being. It was not a friendship—she was too much older than I and too self-involved to give me much in return for my devotion. It was more a Sancho Panza/Knight of La Mancha relationship, with me following her while she explored the power of her youth and beauty.

Vida wanted to be a movie star in Hollywood. That is why she had come to America, she said. I believed that she would be, although she spoke almost no English. That was my job, she said, to teach her to speak perfect English without an accent. She had finished secondary school in her country, and although she was only sixteen, she was not going to school in Paterson. She had other plans. She would get a job as soon as she had papers, save money, then she would leave for Hollywood as soon as possible. She asked me how far Hollywood was. I showed her the state of California in my geography book. She traced a line with her finger from New Jersey to the west coast and smiled. Nothing seemed impossible to Vida.

It was summer when I met Vida, and we spent our days in the small, fenced-in square lot behind our apartment building, avoiding going indoors as much as possible, since it was depressing to Vida to hear her family talking about the need to find jobs, to smell sour baby smells, or to be constantly lectured to by her obese grandmother who sat like a great pile of laundry on a couch all day, watching shows on television which she did not understand. The brother-in-law frightened me a little with his intense eyes and his constant pacing. He spoke in whispers to his wife, Vida's sister, when I was around, as if he did not want me to overhear important matters, making me feel like an intruder. I didn't like to look at Vida's sister. She looked like a Vida who had been left out in the elements for too long: skin stuck to the bones. Vida did not like her family either. When I asked, she said that her mother was dead and that she did not want to speak of the past. Vida thought of only the future.

Once, when we were alone in her apartment, she asked me if I wanted to see her in a bathing suit. She went into the bathroom and emerged in a tight red one-piece suit. She reclined on the bed in a pose she had obviously seen in a magazine. "Do you think I am beautiful?" she asked me. I answered yes, suddenly overwhelmed by a feeling of hopelessness for my skinny body, bony arms and legs, flat chest. "Cadaverous," Vida had once whispered, smiling wickedly into my face after taking my head into her hands and feeling my skull so close to the surface. But right afterwards she had kissed my cheek reassuring me that I would "flesh out" in a few years.

That summer my life shifted on its axis. Until Vida, my mother had been the magnetic force around which all my actions revolved. Since my father was away for long periods of time, my young mother and I had developed a strong symbiotic relationship, with me playing the part of interpreter and buffer to the world for her. I knew at an early age that I would be the one to face landlords, doctors, store clerks, and other "strangers" whose services we needed in my father's absence. English was my weapon and my power. As long as she lived in her fantasy that her exile from Puerto Rico was temporary and that she did not need to learn the language, keeping herself "pure" for her return to the island, then I was in control of our lives outside the realm of our little apartment in Paterson—that is, until Father came home from his Navy tours: then the mantle of responsibility would fall on him. At times, I resented his homecomings, when I would suddenly be thrust back into the role of dependent which I had long ago outgrown—and not by choice.

But Vida changed me. I became secretive, and every outing from our apartment building—to get my mother a pack of L&M's; to buy essentials at the drugstore or supermarket

150

A LAS MUJERES

(which my mother liked to do on an as-needed basis); and, Vida's favorite, to buy Puerto Rican groceries at the bodega—became an adventure with Vida. She was getting restless living in such close quarters with her paranoid sister and brother-in-law. The baby's crying and the pervasive smells of dirty diapers drove her crazy as well as her fat grandmother's lethargy disturbed only by the old woman's need to lecture Vida about her style of dress and her manners, which even my mother had started to comment on.

Vida was modeling herself on the Go-Go girls she loved to watch on dance shows on our television set. She would imitate their movements with me as her audience until we both fell on the sofa laughing. Her eye make-up (bought with my allowance) was dark and heavy, her lips were glossy with iridescent tan lipstick, and her skirts were riding higher and higher on her long legs. When we walked up the street on one of my errands, the men stared; the Puerto Rican men did more than that. More than once we were followed by men inspired to compose *piropos* for Vida—erotically charged words spoken behind us in stage whispers.

I was scared and excited by the trail of Vida's admirers. It was a dangerous game for both of us, but for me especially, since my father could come home unannounced at any time and catch me at it. I was the invisible partner in Vida's life; I was her little pocket mirror she could take out any time to confirm her beauty and her power. But I was too young to think in those terms, all I knew was the thrill of being in her company, being touched by her magical powers of transformation that could make a walk to the store a deliciously sinful escapade.

Then Vida fell in love. He was, in my jealous eyes, a Neanderthal, a big hairy man who drove a large black Oldsmobile recklessly around our block hour after hour just to catch a glimpse of Vida. He had promised to drive her to California, she confided to me. Then she started to use me as cover in order to meet him, asking me to take a walk with her, then leaving me to wait on a park bench or at the library for what seemed an eternity while she drove around with her muscle-bound lover. I became disenchanted with Vida, but remained loyal to her throughout the summer. Once in a while we still shared a good time. She loved to tell me in detail about her "romance." Apparently, she was not totally naive, and had managed to keep their passionate encounters within the limits of kissing and petting in the spacious backseat of the black Oldsmobile. But he was getting impatient, she told me, so she had decided to announce her engagement to her family soon. They would get married and go to California together. He would be her manager and protect her from the Hollywood "wolves."

By this time I was getting weary of Vida's illusions about Hollywood. I was glad when school started in the fall and I got into my starched blue jumper only to discover that it was too tight and too short for me. I had "developed" over the summer.

Life settled to our normal routine when we were in the States. This was: my brother and I went to Catholic school and did our lessons, our mother waited for our father to come home on leave from his Navy tours, and all of us waited to hear when we would be returning to Puerto Rico— which was usually every time Father went to Europe, every six months or so. Vida would sometimes come down to our apartment and complain bitterly about life with her family upstairs. They had absolutely refused to accept her fiancé. They were making plans to migrate elsewhere. She did not have work papers yet, but did not want to go with them. She would have to find a place to stay until she got married. She began courting my mother. I would come home to find them looking at bride magazines and laughing together. Vida hardly spoke to me at all.

Father came home in his winter blues and everything

152

changed for us. I felt the almost physical release of the burden of responsibility for my family and allowed myself to spend more time doing what I like to do best of all—read. It was a solitary life we led in Paterson, New Jersey, and both my brother and I became avid readers. My mother did too, although because she had little English, her fare was made up of Corín Tellado romances, which Schulze's drugstore carried, and the *Buenhogar* and *Vanidades* magazines that she received in the mail occasionally. But she read less and I more when Father came home. The ebb and flow of this routine was interrupted by Vida that year. With my mother's help she introduced herself into our family.

Father, normally a reticent man, suspicious of strangers by nature, and always vigilant about dangers to his children, also fell under Vida's spell. Amazingly, he agreed to let her come stay in our apartment until her wedding some months away. She moved into my room. She slept on what had been my little brother's twin bed until he got his own room, a place where I liked to keep my collection of dolls from around the world that my father had sent me. These had to be put in a box in the dark closet now.

Vida's perfume took over my room. As soon as I walked in, I smelled her. It got on my clothes. The nuns at my school commented on it since we were not allowed to use perfume or cosmetics. I tried to wash it off, but it was strong and pervasive. Vida tried to win me by taking me shopping. She was getting money from her boyfriend—for her trousseau—she said. She bought me a tight black skirt just like hers and a pair of shoes with heels. When she had me model it for my family, my father frowned and left the room silently. I was not allowed to keep the things. Since the man was never seen at our house, we did not know that Vida had broken the engagement and was seeing other men.

My mother started to complain about little things Vida did, or did not do. She did not help with housework, although she did contribute money. Where was she getting it? She did not bathe daily (a major infraction in my mother's eyes), but poured cologne over herself in quantities. She claimed to be at church too many times a week and came home smelling of alcohol, even though it was hard to tell because of the perfume. Mother was spreading her wings and getting ready to fight for exclusivity over her nest.

But, Father, surprising us all again, argued for fairness for the señorita—my mother made a funny "harrump" noise at that word, which in Spanish connotes virginity and purity. He said we had promised her asylum until she got settled and it was important that we send her out of our house in a respectable manner: married, if possible. He liked playing cards with her. She was cunning and smart, a worthy adversary.

Mother fumed. My brother and I spent a lot of time in the kitchen or living room, reading where the air was not saturated with "Evening in Paris."

Vida was changing. After a few months, she no longer spoke of Hollywood; she barely spoke to me at all. She got her papers and got a job in a factory sewing dungarees. Then, almost as suddenly as she had come into my life, she disappeared.

One afternoon I came home to find my mother mopping the floors strenuously with a pine cleaner, giving the apartment the kind of thorough scrubbing usually done as a family effort in the spring. When I went into my room the dolls were back in their former place on the extra bed. No sign of Vida.

I don't remember discussing her parting much. Although my parents were fair, they did not always feel the need to explain or justify their decisions to us. I have always believed that my mother simply demanded her territory, fearing the growing threat of Vida's beauty and erotic slovenliness that was permeating her clean home. Or perhaps Vida found life with us as stifling as she had with her family. If I had been a little older, I would have learned more from Vida, but she came at a time when I needed security more than knowledge of human nature. She was a fascinating creature.

The last time I saw Vida's face it was on a poster. It announced her crowning as a beauty queen for a Catholic church in another parish. Beauty contests were held by churches as fundraisers at that time, as contradictory as that seems to me now: a church sponsoring a competition to choose the most physically attractive female in the congregation. I still feel that it was right to see Vida wearing the little tiara of fake diamonds in that photograph with the caption underneath: Vida wins!

María

by Amina Muñoz

I have a picture of her
standing on the roof
next to the clothesline,
smiling.
Empty beer cans
and glue tubes
are at her feet
and her face
is wearing the same expression
as the cracked linoleum
we would mop and wax every weekend
while water balloons splattered below
on the 96 degree sidewalk
and the kitchen table
slipped in its own grease.

To a Woman I Love

by Cristina González

¡Qué eres fea, me dicen,
medio india,
difícil mexicana!
¡Qué eres mujer terrible!

¿Y qué de la gracia
de tus rizos de viento,
de tu poncho tapamundos,
de tus multiples acentos?

¿Serás mujer terrible
por fumar tabaco negro
por beber whisky y tequila,
por tus norma-tivos versos?

Es cierto que tienes algo
de imponente y monumental,
let me tell you.
Te veo como una diosa piramidal,
bien afincada en el suelo,
bien apuntado hacia el cielo.
También tienes algo de faro.

A veces me parece que tus rizos
son destellos,
porque BRILLAS,
en tanto que ellos . . .
Oh, dear!
En sus cúbicas cabezas
la luz brilla por su ausencia.

A VANESSA

by Elsa Zambosco

Me miras Vanessa
con tanta dulzura,
tu cara, blancura
y tu rubia cabeza,
que siento que espesa
la sangre me corre,
y no hay quien borre
tu beso de fresa.
Y no es sopresa
que te quiera tanto,
ni que piense cuanto
tienes de riqueza.
Me basta con esa
sonrisa tan tuya
que no hay quien huya
ni vea simpleza.
Y te sientes presa
de mi amor naciente,
y ni estás consciente
que ya eres princesa.

from Silent Dancing

María Sabida

by Judith Ortiz Cofer

Once upon a time there lived a girl who was so smart that she was known throughout Puerto Rico as María Sabida. María Sabida came into the world with her eyes open. They say that at the moment of her birth she spoke to the attending midwife and told her what herbs to use to make a special *guarapo*, a tea that would put her mother back on her feet immediately. They say that the two women would have thought the infant was possessed if María Sabida had not convinced them with her descriptions of life in heaven that she was touched by God and not spawned by the Devil.

María Sabida grew up in the days when the King of Spain owned Puerto Rico, but had forgotten to send law and justice to this little island lost on the map of the world. And so thieves and murderers roamed the land terrorizing the poor people. By the time María Sabida was of marriageable age, one such *ladrón* had taken over the district where she lived.

For years people had been subjected to abuse from this evil man and his henchmen. He robbed them of their cattle and then made them buy their own cows back from him. He would take their best chickens and produce when he came into town on Saturday afternoons riding with his men through the stalls set up by farmers. Overturning their tables, he would yell, "Put it on my account." But of course he never paid for anything he took. One year several little children disappeared while walking to the river, and although the townspeople searched and searched, no trace of them was ever found. That is when María Sabida entered the picture. She was fifteen then, and a beautiful girl with the courage of a man, they say.

She watched the chief *ladrón* the next time he rampaged through the pueblo. She saw that he was a young man: red-skinned, and tough as leather. *Cuero y sangre, nada más*, she said to herself, a man of flesh and blood. And so she prepared herself to either conquer or to kill this man.

María Sabida followed the horses' trail deep into the woods. Though she left the town far behind she never felt afraid or lost. María Sabida could read the sun, the moon, and the stars for direction. When she got hungry, she knew which fruits were good to eat, which roots and leaves were poisonous, and how to follow the footprints of animals to a waterhole. At nightfall, María Sabida came to the edge of a clearing where a large house, almost like a fortress, stood in the forest.

"No woman has ever set foot in that house," she thought, "no *casa* is this, but a man-place." It was a house built for violence, with no windows on the ground level, but there were turrets on the roof where men could stand guard with guns. She waited until it was nearly dark and approached the house through the kitchen side. She found it by smell.

In the kitchen which she knew would have to have a door or window for ventilation, she saw an old man stirring a huge pot. Out of the pot stuck little arms and legs. Angered by the sight, María Sabida entered the kitchen, pushed the old man aside, and picking up the pot threw its horrible contents out of the window.

"Witch, witch, what have you done with my master's stew!" yelled the old man. "He will kill us both when he gets home and finds his dinner spoiled."

"Get, you filthy *viejo*." María Sabida grabbed the old man's beard and pulled him to his feet. "Your master will have the best dinner of his life if you follow my instructions."

María Sabida then proceeded to make the most delicious *asopao* the old man had ever tasted, but she would answer no questions about herself, except to say that she was his master's fiancé.

When the meal was done, María Sabida stretched and yawned and said that she would go upstairs and rest until her *prometido* came home. Then she went upstairs and waited.

The men came home and ate ravenously of the food María Sabida had cooked. When the chief *ladrón* had praised the old man for a fine meal, the cook admitted that it had been *la prometida* who had made the tasty chicken stew.

"My what?" the leader roared, "I have no *prometida*." And he and his men ran upstairs. But there were many floors, and by the time they were halfway to the room where María Sabida waited, many of the men had dropped down unconscious and the others had slowed down to a crawl until they too were overcome with irresistible sleepiness. Only the chief *ladrón* made it to where María Sabida awaited him holding a paddle that she had found among his weapons. Fighting to keep his eyes open, he asked her, "Who are you, and why have you poisoned me?"

"I am your future wife, María Sabida, and you are not poisoned, I added a special sleeping powder that tastes like oregano to your *asopao*. You will not die."

"Witch!" yelled the chief *ladrón* "I will kill you. Don't you know who I am?" And reaching for her, he fell on his knees, whereupon María Sabida beat him with the paddle until he lay curled like a child on the floor. Each time he tried to attack her, she beat him some more. When she was satisfied that he was vanquished, María Sabida left the house and went back to town.

A week later, the chief *ladrón* rode into town with his men again. By then everyone knew what María Sabida had done and they were afraid of what these evil men would do in retribution. "Why did you not just kill him when you had a chance, *muchacha*?" many of the townswomen had asked María Sabida. But she had just answered mysteriously, "It is better to conquer than to kill." The townspeople then barricaded themselves behind closed doors when they heard the pounding of the thieves' horses approaching. But the gang did not stop until they arrived at María Sabida's house. There the men, instead of guns, brought out musical instruments: a *cuatro*, a *güiro*, *maracas*, and a harmonica. Then they played a lovely melody.

"María Sabida, María Sabida, my strong and wise María," called out the leader, sitting tall on his horse under María Sabida's window, "come out and listen to a song I've written for you—I call it *The Ballad of María Sabida*."

María Sabida then appeared on her balcony wearing a wedding dress. The chief *ladrón* sang his song to her: a lively tune about a woman who had the courage of a man and the wisdom of a judge, who had conquered the heart of the best *bandido* on the island of Puerto Rico. He had a strong voice and all the people cowering in their locked houses heard his tribute to María Sabida and crossed themselves at the miracle she had wrought.

One by one they all came out and soon María Sabida's front yard was full of people singing and dancing. The *ladrones* had come prepared with casks of wine, bottles of rum, and a wedding cake made by the old cook from the tender meat of coconuts. The leader of the thieves and María Sabida were married on that day. But all had not yet been settled between them. That evening, as she rode behind him on his horse, she felt the dagger concealed beneath his clothes. She knew then that she had not fully won the battle for this man's heart.

On her wedding night María Sabida suspected that her husband wanted to kill her. After their dinner, which the man had insisted on cooking himself, they went upstairs. María Sabida asked for a little time alone to prepare herself. He said he would take a walk but would return very soon. When she heard him leave the house, María Sabida went down to the kitchen and took several gallons of honey from the pantry. She went back to the bedroom and there she fashioned a life-sized doll out of her clothes and poured

162

A LAS MUJERES

the honey into it. She then blew out the candle, covered the figure with a sheet and hid herself under the bed.

After a short time, she heard her husband climbing the stairs. He tip-toed into the dark room thinking her asleep in their marriage bed. Peeking out from under the bed, María Sabida saw the glint of the knife her husband pulled out from inside his shirt. Like a fierce panther he leapt onto the bed and stabbed the doll's body over and over with his dagger. Honey splattered his face and fell on his lips. Shocked, the man jumped off the bed and licked his lips.

"How sweet is my wife's blood. How sweet is María Sabida in death—how sour in life and how sweet in death. If I had known she was so sweet, I would not have murdered her." And so declaring, he kneeled down on the floor beside the bed and prayed to María Sabida's soul for forgiveness.

At that moment María Sabida came out of her hiding place. "Husband, I have tricked you once more, I am not dead." In his joy, the man threw down his knife and embraced María Sabida, swearing that he would never kill or steal again. And he kept his word, becoming in later years an honest farmer. Many years later he was elected mayor of the same town he had once terrorized with his gang of *ladrones*.

María Sabida made a real *casa* out of his thieves' den, and they had many children together, all of whom could speak at birth. But, they say, María Sabida always slept with one eye open, and that is why she lived to be one hundred years old and wiser than any other woman on the Island of Puerto Rico, and her name was known even in Spain.

CHAPTER 7

EL BARRIO

El Barrio, My Home

by Edna Robles

The book *Nilda* is about an Hispanic girl, her struggles, her hopes and especially about her being brought up in El Barrio . . . which isn't that bad — I am being brought up there myself.

I can understand that being brought up in El Barrio is not an easy thing. Some people tend to judge it by what they hear other people say. It's very hard to grow up and be a success when people assume that human beings from "that place," El Barrio, are all junkies and don't know the first thing about education. Of course, they are very wrong. They tend to think that just because you come from El Barrio, or another "bad" neighborhood, and are Hispanic, and especially if you are a female, you're not worth much. They also think you are low in education. This bothers me so much.

You have to live in a place and then, and only then, can you judge it.

El Barrio

by Luz Otero

I live on 100th Street between Second and First Avenues. That area where I live is totally hooked on drugs. I know this because everywhere I go there is always someone who is sleeping on the hallway floor or on the stairs inside the building. Sometimes I catch someone behind the stairs smoking marijuana or sniffing crack. I used to watch police come in the night, running after those people they found with drugs. After they caught them, I heard the police scream at the drug addicts to follow the police orders. I never was really scared. I didn't care.

This changed all of a sudden.

Last June my mother bought airline tickets so that we could go to Puerto Rico because my grandmother was very sick. My mother had almost all the suitcases packed, but there was one more that we needed. She remembered that she had bought one and left it on lay-away. So the next day she sent me and my brother to pay all the money at the store and get her suitcase.

I had to walk with my brother all the way to 116th Street to get the suitcase. Just as we returned to our building, I rang the intercom and told my mother to ring the buzzer so that we could get in. She screamed, "¡Empuja la puerta! ¡El timbre no trabaja!" At that moment a tall, dirty, drug-addicted-looking man pushed the door so hard that the sound made me deaf! I wasn't scared just because he wasn't from my building—I thought he was going to visit someone. I kept on walking, I didn't care. He asked me, "Does the elevator work?" And I said, "No."

As I carried the suitcase, my brother and I were talking about how it was going to be in Puerto Rico. The man climbed the stairs behind us. As the man, my brother and I reached the second floor, he took out a knife and grabbed my brother's hand. My mind went blank, and I totally didn't know what was going on! The man said in a nasty way, "Give me the chain and the bracelet BOY!" My brother said, "No, stop, come on!"

Suddenly my mind came to life again, and I ran up the stairs and banged on my mother's door. When my mother opened the door, I was so nervous and crying I couldn't even call the police or tell my mother what happened. And after a while I got worse because I remembered that I left my brother, José, downstairs. I felt so bad because I thought that he was already dead. My mother told me to call the police (she only speaks a little bit of English) and tell the whole story. At first, since I sounded young on the phone, the police thought I was fooling around. But when I told them my address and told them it was an emergency, they believed me, and they were on their way.

While they were on their way, I told my mother what happened, and she was screaming as if they had murdered my brother. Suddenly there was a knock on the door. I was so happy because it was my brother, but my mother and I thought that the man was using him so that we could serve him as hostages. My brother was saying, "¡Mami, abre la puerta, el hombre no está aquí!"

And my mother said "¿Estás seguro?"

My brother said, "Yes, ma, estoy seguro."

When my mother opened the door, I saw that my brother was very worried, and I noticed that his necklace was gone. The only thing that was there were the scratches of the stupid man.

A policeman came and took us to the police station. With my mother, he made a report and gave us an appointment so that the next time we met we could go around in a detective car to see if we could recognize the man. The detective's name was Horne. He was nice and made us feel sure of ourselves again.

After a while, on July the first, they caught the man, and wasn't that a relief! But after this happened, my brother and I have been afraid of our neighborhood. Now I usually don't go to the store for my mother anymore. I mean, before this happened, I stayed out at night until at least 9:00 p.m. Not anymore. I am also very scared of the drug addicts that stay in my building, sleeping or taking drugs in front of me or other people.

Once my mother and I came from the store and when we entered the building, we saw a lady, all loaded and her face burned. She had a small, silver pocket knife. I told my mother, "Mom, I'm not entering the building." And she said, "Don't worry, she won't do anything to us."

When we were going to go up the stairs, she looked at us as if she wanted to kill somebody. Then we got closer to her, and I got so scared that I ran up the stairs. The lady started screaming, saying, "Why does everybody have to be scared of me, I'm not a monster!" Meanwhile, I was saying to myself, from using all those drugs, your face looks like you are a monster.

I hope that one of these days this fear will go away. As I get more and more scared of my neighborhood, I'm getting more and more fearful of other people.

Braces and Intelligence

by Shanique García

Though braces and intelligence may seem like stupid concerns, they can cause problems for some of us in Harlem. And that's the truth. Almost everyone in Harlem who wears braces is verbally or physically harassed. I know I am. I am constantly called "metal mouth," and people often talk about how they would like to put my head in an electrical socket in order to electrocute me. People also ask me quite often if I can feel soundwaves conducted through metal when I listen to the radio. Well, the answer is no!!

Another problem in Harlem is that if you are smart and don't dress or look like the "fly" people, you will usually be talked about, harassed, or beaten up. Most of the time, people ask what school I attend and call me a nerd and say no wonder I wear braces. Maybe I am a little smart and have braces, but so what!!

Just stop dogging me around!!

Do It To The Music

by Carmen Martin

The loud sounds of a heavy bass song telling a story fill the streets of Spanish Harlem. As usual, there are different groups of people hanging outside in the streets, claiming their own territories. Different types of music fill the air—music passed down from generation to generation—from the Caribbean-Puerto Rican style to the new rough cut hip-hop tunes.

All these musical styles have something in common, they all tell a story. Sometimes the stories tell about good things that happened, but most of the time they tell of bad things. The truth is said to be heard in these songs—the truth about life, both the lows (the dead, the murdered, the raped, the drug dealers, the drunks, the homeless, and most important, the changes in the neighborhood) and the highs (the action, the streets always alive with feeling, the family feeling of knowing everyone in your building and on your block, a neighborhood that never sleeps.)

Spanish Harlem is always thought to be such a bad area. The crime, the drugs, the poverty. And it's true, all of this has helped to bring it down. But there is something you can't take away from it — its people and their love for music. On the hard, long days when even the last soul wants to give up, coming home to listen to the tunes of life helps you relax. On long summer days, sitting outside with the late afternoon breeze, having a cool drink and just listening to the tunes make you move all around, dance in the streets, sweat and forget your landlord raised the rent and you can't pay.

Music has its special vibes. It makes you feel safe. And in a place that has been stricken by poverty and crime, anything that gets you carried away puts a smile on your face. Music is a way to escape for people everywhere. Just listen a little and keep open minded. You'll hear and feel the message that music brings.

from El Bronx Remembered

A Very Special Pet

by Nicholasa Mohr

The Fernández family kept two pets in their small five-room apartment. One was a large female alley cat who was a good mouser when she wasn't in heat. She was very large and had a rich coat of grey fur with black stripes and a long bushy tail. Her eyes were yellow and she had long white whiskers. Her name was Marialú.

If they would listen carefully to what Marialú said, Mrs. Fernández assured the children, they would hear her calling her husband Raúl.

"Raúl . . . "Raúl . . . this is Marialú. . . "Raúl . . . "Raúl . . . this is Marialú," the children would sing loudly. They all felt sorry for Marialú, because no matter how long and how hard she howled, or how many times she ran off, she could never find her real husband, "Raúl.

The second pet was not really supposed to be a pet at all. She was a small, skinny white hen with a red crest and a yellow beak. Graciela and Eugenio Fernández had bought her two years ago, to provide them and their eight children with good fresh eggs. Her name was Joncrofo, after Graciela Fernández's favorite Hollywood movie star, Joan Crawford. People would repeat the hen's name as she pronounced it, "Joncrofo la gallina."

Joncrofo la gallina lived in the kitchen. She had one foot tied with a very long piece of twine to one of the legs of the kitchen sink. The twine was long enough for Joncrofo to wander all over the kitchen and even to hop onto the large window with the fire escape. Under the sink Mrs. Fernández kept clean newspapers, water, and cornmeal for the hen, and a wooden box lined with some soft flannel cloth and packing straw. It was there that they hoped Joncrofo would lay her eggs. The little hen slept and rested there, but perhaps because she was nervous, she had never once laid an egg.

Graciela and Eugenio Fernández had come to the Bronx six years ago and moved into the small apartment. Except for a trip once before to the seaport city of Mayagüez in Puerto Rico, they had never left their tiny village in the mountains. To finance their voyage to New York, Mr. and Mrs. Fernández had sold their small plot of land, the little livestock they had, and their wooden cabin. The sale had provided the fare and expenses for them and their five children. Since then, three more children had been born. City life was foreign to them, and they had to learn everything, even how to get on a subway and travel. Graciela Fernández had been terribly frightened at first of the underground trains, traffic, and large crowds of people. Although she finally adjusted, she still confined herself to the apartment and seldom went out.

She would never complain; she would pray at the small altar she had set up in the kitchen, light her candles and murmur that God would provide and not forget her and her family. She was proud of the fact that they did not have to ask for welfare or home relief, as so many other families did.

"Papi provides for us. We are lucky and we have to thank Jesus Christ," she would say, making the sign of the cross.

Eugenio Fernández had found a job as a porter in one of the large buildings in the garment center in Manhattan. He still held the same job, but he hoped to be promoted someday to freight elevator operator. In the meantime, he sold newspapers and coffee on the side, ran errands for people in the building, and was always available for extra work. Still, the money he brought home was barely enough to support ten people.

"Someday I'm gonna get that job. I got my eye on it, and Mr. Friedlander, he likes me . . . so we gotta be patient. Besides the increase in salary, my God!—I could do a million things on the side, and we could make a lot of money. Why I could . . ." Mr. Fernández would tell his family this story several times a week.

"Oh, wow! Papi, we are gonna be rich when you get that job!" the children would shriek.

"Can we get a television when we get rich, Papi?" Pablito, the oldest boy, would ask. Nellie, Carmen, and Linda wanted a telephone.

"Everybody on the block got a telephone but us." Nellie, the oldest girl, would speak for them.

The younger children, William, Olgita, and Freddie, would request lots of toys and treats. Baby Nancy would smile and babble happily with everybody.

"We gonna get everything and we gonna leave El Bronx," Mr. Fernández would assure them. "We even gonna save enough to buy our farm in Puerto Rico—a big one! With lots of land, maybe a hundred acres, and a chicken house, pigs, goats, even a cow. We can plant coffee and some sugar, and have all the fruit trees—mangoes, sweet oranges, everything!" Mr. Fernández would pause and tell the children all about the wonderful food they could eat back home in his village. "All you need to get the farm is a good start."

"We gonna take Joncrofo, right?" the kids would ask. And Marialú? Her too?"

"Sure," Mr. Fernández would say good-naturedly, "even Raúl, her husband, when she finds him, eh?" He would wink, laughing. "And Joncrofo don't have to be tied up like a prisoner no more—she could run loose."

It was the dream of Graciela and Eugenio Fernández to go back to their village as owners of their own farm, with the faith that the land would provide for them.

This morning Mrs. Fernández sat in her kitchen, thinking that things were just not going well. Now that the holidays were coming and Christmas would soon be here, money was scarcer than ever and prices were higher than ever. Things had been bad for Eugenio Fernández ; he was still working as a porter and lately had been sick with a bad throat. They had not saved one cent toward their farm. In fact, they still owed the dry-goods salesman for the kitchen curtains and two bedspreads; even insurance payments were long overdue. She wanted to find a job and help out, but there were still three small preschool children at home to care for. Lately, she had begun to worry; it was hard to put meat on the table.

Graciela Fernández sighed, looking about her small, clean kitchen, and caught sight of Joncrofo running frantically after a stray cockroach. The hen quickly jerked her neck and snapped up the insect with her beak. In spite of all the fumigation and the daily scrubbing, it seemed there was always a cockroach or two in sight. Joncrofo was always searching for a tasty morsel—spiders, ants, even houseflies. She was quick and usually got her victim.

The little white hen had a wicked temper and would snap at anyone she felt was annoying her. Even Marialú knew better; she had a permanent scar on her right ear as a result of Joncrofo's sharp yellow beak. Now the cat carefully kept her distance.

In spite of Joncrofo's cantankerous ways, the children loved her. They were proud of her because no one else on the block had such a pet. Whenever other children teased them about not having a television, the Fernández children would remind them that Joncrofo was a very special pet. Even Baby Nancy would laugh and clap when she saw Joncrofo rushing toward one of her tiny victims.

For some time now, Mrs. Fernández had given up any hope of Joncrofo producing eggs and had also accepted her as a house pet. She had tried everything: warm milk, fresh

176

EL BARRIO

grass from the park, relining the wooden box. She had even consulted the spiritualist and followed the instructions faithfully, giving the little hen certain herbs to eat and reciting the prayers; and yet nothing ever worked. She had even tried to fatten her up, but the more Joncrofo ate, it seemed, the less she gained.

After thinking about it for several days, this morning Graciela Fernández reached her decision. Tonight, her husband would have good fresh chicken broth for his cold, and her children a full plate of rice with chicken. This silly hen was really no use alive to anyone, she concluded.

It had been six long years since Mrs. Fernández had killed a chicken, but she still remembered how. She was grateful that the older children were in school, and somehow she would find a way to keep the three younger ones at the other end of the apartment.

Very slowly she got up and found the kitchen cleaver. Feeling it with her thumb, she decided it should be sharper, and taking a flat stone, she carefully sharpened the edge as she planned the best way to finish off the hen.

It was still quite early. If she worked things right, she could be through by noontime and have supper ready before her husband got home. She would tell the children that Joncrofo flew away. Someone had untied the twine on her foot and when she opened the window to the fire escape to bring in the mop, Joncrofo flew out and disappeared. That's it, she said to herself, satisfied.

The cleaver was sharp enough and the small chopping block was set up on the kitchen sink. Mrs. Fernández bent down and looked Joncrofo right in the eye. The hen stared back without any fear or much interest. Good, thought Mrs. Fernández, and she walked back into the apartment where Olgita, Freddie, and Baby Nancy were playing.

"I'm going to clean the kitchen, and I don't want you to come inside. Understand?" The children looked at her and nodded. "I mean it—you stay here. If I catch you coming to the kitchen when I am cleaning, you get it with this," she said, holding out her hand with an open palm, gesturing as if she were spanking them. "Now, I'm going to put the chair across the kitchen entrance so that Baby Nancy can't come in. O.K.?" The children nodded again. Their mother very often put one of the kitchen chairs across the kitchen entrance so the baby could not come inside. "Now," she said, "you listen and you stay here!" The children began to play, interested only in their game.

Mrs. Fernández returned to the kitchen, smoothed down her hair, readjusted her apron, and rolled up her sleeves. She put one of the chairs across the threshold to block the entrance, then found a couple of extra rags and old newspapers.

"Joncrofo," she whispered and walked over to the hen. To her surprise, the hen ran under the sink and sat in her box. Mrs. Fernández bent down, but before she could grab her, Joncrofo jumped out of her box and slid behind one of the legs of the kitchen sink. She extended her hand and felt the hen's sharp beak nip one of her fingers. "Ave Maria!" she said, pulling away and putting the injured finger in her mouth. "O.K., you wanna play games. You dumb hen!"

She decided to untie the twine that was tied to the leg of the sink and then pull the hen toward her. Taking a large rag, she draped it over one hand and then, bending down once more, untied the twine and began to pull. Joncrofo resisted, and Mrs. Fernández pulled. Harder and harder she tugged and pulled, at the same time making sure she held the rag securely, so that she could protect herself against Joncrofo's sharp beak. Quickly she pulled, and with one fast jerk of the twine, the hen was up in the air. Quickly Mrs. Fernández draped the rag over the hen. Frantically, Joncrofo began to cackle and jump, flapping her wings and snapping her beak. Mrs. Fernández found herself spinning as she struggled to hold on to Joncrofo, who kept wriggling

EL BARRIO

and jumping. With great effort, Joncrofo got her head loose and sank her beak into Mrs. Fernández's arm. In an instant she released the hen.

Joncrofo ran around the kitchen cackling loudly, flapping her wings and ruffling her feathers. The hen kept an eye on Mrs. Fernández , who also watched her as she held on to her injured arm. White feathers were all over the kitchen; some still floated softly in the air.

Each time Mrs. Fernández went toward Joncrofo, she fled swiftly, cackling even louder and snapping wildly with her beak.

Mrs. Fernández remained still for a moment, then went over to the far end of the kitchen and grabbed a broom. Using the handle, she began to hit the hen, swatting her back and forth like a tennis ball. Joncrofo kept running and trying to dodge the blows, but Mrs. Fernández kept landing the broom each time. The hen began to lose her footing, and Mrs. Fernández vigorously swung the broom, hitting the small white hen until her cackle became softer and softer. Not able to stand any longer, Joncrofo wobbled, moving with slow jerky movements, and dropped to the floor. Mrs. Fernández let go of the broom and rushed over to the hen. Grabbing her by the neck, she lifted her into the air and spun her around a few times, dropping her on the floor. Near exhaustion, Mrs. Fernández could hear her own heavy breathing.

"Mami . . . Mamita. What are you doing to Joncrofo?"

Turning, she saw Olgita, Freddie, and Baby Nancy staring at her wide-eyed. "Ma . . . Mami . . . what are you doing to Joncrofo?" they shouted and began to cry. In her excitement, Mrs. Fernández had forgotten completely about the children and the noise the hen had made.

"Oooo . . . is she dead?" Olgita cried, pointing. "Is she dead?" She began to whine.

"You killed Joncrofo, Mami! You killed her. She's dead."

Freddie joined his sister, sobbing loudly. Baby Nancy watched her brother and sister and began to cry too. Shrieking, she threw herself on the floor in a tantrum.

"You killed her! You're bad, Mami. You're bad," screamed Olgita.

"Joncrofo . . . I want Joncrofo. . . ." Freddie sobbed. "I'm gonna tell Papi," he screamed, choking with tears.

"Me too! I'm gonna tell too," cried Olgita. "I'm telling Nellie, and she'll tell her teacher on you," she yelled.

Mrs. Fernández watched her children as they stood looking in at her, barricaded by the chair. Then she looked down at the floor where Joncrofo lay, perfectly still. Walking over to the chair, she removed it from the entrance, and before she could say anything, the children ran to the back of the apartment, still yelling and crying.

"Joncrofo . . . We want Joncrofo . . . You're bad . . . you're bad. . . ."

Mrs. Fernández felt completely helpless as she looked about her kitchen. What a mess she thought! Things were overturned, and there were white feathers everywhere. Feeling the tears coming to her eyes, she sat down and began to cry quietly. What's the use now? She sighed and thought, I should have taken her to the butcher. He would have done it for a small fee. Oh, this life, she said to herself, wiping her eyes. Now my children hate me. She remembered that when she was just about Olgita's age she was already helping her mother kill chickens and never thought much about slaughtering animals for food.

Graciela Fernández took a deep breath and began to wonder what she would do with Joncrofo now that she was dead. No use cooking her. They won't eat her, she thought, shaking her head. As she contemplated what was to be done, she heard a low grunt. Joncrofo was still alive!

Mrs. Fernández reached under the sink and pulled out the wooden box. She put the large rag into the box and placed the hen inside. Quickly she went over to a cabinet and took out an eyedropper, filling it with water. Then she forced open Joncrofo's beak and dropped some water inside. She put a washcloth into lukewarm water and washed down the hen, smoothing her feathers.

"Joncrofo," she cooed softly, "cro . . . cro . . . Joncrofita," and stroked the hen gently. The hen was still breathing, but her eyes were closed. Mrs. Fernández went over to the cupboard and pulled out a small bottle of rum that Mr. Fernández saved only for special occasions and for guests. She gave some to Joncrofo. The hen opened her eyes and shook her head, emitting a croaking sound.

"What a good little hen," said Mrs. Fernández. "That's right, come on . . . come, wake up, and I'll give you something special. How about if I give you some nice dry corn? . . . Come on." She continued to pet the hen and talk sweetly to her. Slowly, Joncrofo opened her beak and tried to cackle, and again she made a croaking sound. Blinking her eyes, she sat up in her box, ruffled her feathers, and managed a low soft cackle.

"Is she gonna live, Mami?" Mrs. Fernández turned and saw Olgita, Freddie, and Baby Nancy standing beside her.

"Of course she's going to live. What did you think I did, kill her? Tsk, tsk . . . did you really think that? You are all very silly children," she said, and shook her finger at them. They stared back at her with bewilderment, not speaking. "All that screaming at me was not nice." She went on, "I was only trying to save her. Joncrofo got very sick, and see?" She held up the eyedropper. "I had to help her get well. I had to catch her in order to cure her. Understand?"

Olgita and Freddie looked at each other and then at their mother.

"When I saw that she was getting sick, I had to catch her. She was running all around, jumping and going crazy. Yes." Mrs. Fernández opened her eyes and pointed to her head, making a circular movement with her right index finger. "She went cuckoo! If I didn't stop her, Joncrofo would have really killed herself," she said earnestly. "So I gave her some medicine—and now . . ."

"Is that why you got her drunk, Mami?" interrupted Olgita.

"What?" asked Mrs. Fernández.

"You gave her Papi's rum . . . in the eyedropper. We seen you," Freddie said. Olgita nodded.

"Well," Mrs. Fernandez said, "that don't make her drunk. It . . . it . . . ah . . . just calms her down. Sometimes it's used like a medicine."

"And it makes her happy again?" Olgita asked. "Like Papi? He always gets happy when he drinks some."

"Yes, that's right. You're right. To make Joncrofo happy again," Mrs. Fernández said.

"Why did she get sick, Mami, and go crazy?" asked Freddie.

"I don't know why. Those things just happen," Mrs. Fernández responded.

"Do them things happen on the farm in Puerto Rico?"

"That's right," she said. "Now let me be. I gotta finish cleaning here. Go on, go to the back of the house; take Baby Nancy . . . go on."

The children left the kitchen, and Mrs. Fernández barricaded the entrance once more. She picked up the box with Joncrofo, who sat quietly blinking, and shoved it under the sink. Then she put the cleaver and the chopping board away. Picking up the broom, she began to sweep the feathers and torn newspapers that were strewn all about the kitchen.

In the back of the apartment, where the children played, they could hear their mother singing a familiar song. It was about a beautiful island where the tall green palm trees swayed under a golden sky and the flowers were always in bloom.

CHAPTER 8

PREJUDICE

Different Perspectives

by Edna Robles

I want to say something that's meaningful to me, but it is hard because I don't know how to put it into words.

What I want to say is that Hispanic women aren't the only ones that have problems of prejudice. Black, immigrant, and even white women have these problems, too. I guess we all think we are the only ones who suffer from prejudice, when we are not. This makes us all a little weird, because if we are all suffering from some kind of prejudice, we must all be practicing it too, in some way!

The problem is that we all look at things from different perspectives . . . but from only one perspective.

Remembering Zebras

by María Persons

Beginning in second grade, I went to a very good public elementary school, and I had a lot of friends there. Most of the children that went there were kind of rich and white. Usually that doesn't bother me. To be truthful, when I meet someone I don't right away think, Oh she's white! or Oh, he is black! And I really haven't been faced with much prejudice.

But I do remember when I was in second grade when Rena and I were partners on line (it was the second grade so, of course, we had to take partners). We were on our way across the cafeteria when she told me that she was happy that I was white because her parents didn't like blacks. I knew that I should have said something but at that time it didn't seem right. I guess that was the only time I faced racism, and I consider myself very lucky for this reason.

Or is it that I don't want to remember those other times when I had to face prejudice?

When I do think about it, there is another incident that I just can't figure out. I live in Ruppert Towers on the East Side of Manhattan. My family has been living there for about eleven years, so of course we have some really close friends, like Richard and Martin Layton. They have been around as long as I can remember. They're my brother's (who is right now fifteen years old) best friends. Richard, who is the older one of the two, is now a sophomore in high school. He has always been like the leader. Whatever he said went. Martin is a freshman in high school, like my brother. I remember so many times going to Great Adventure with them, going on vacation for a week with them at the Jersey Shore. We had once tried to make the Guinness Book of World Records and jumped on my mother's bed for five hours.

But I also remember one time, when I was in fourth grade,

186

Prejudice

and we were all in the playground. Richard and Martin started calling me and my brothers zebras. A zebra is someone with one parent who is white and one parent who is black. We told them we were not zebras because our mom is Hispanic, not white. But then they said Hispanic means your nationality and not our skin color. I was around nine years old, and I had known them all my life, so anything they said went. What they said made me feel differently about myself, because after that, whenever anyone would ask me my nationality, I would not know what to say.

Which Line Is This? I Forget

by Lorna Dee Cervantes

What a fools game I'm playing,
this foolish game called
"Shame."
Where the rules are rigid
and the stakes are high
and you play for keeps.
Constantly running,
lying,
making up lies to cover my lies,
pretending,
hiding from something I know nothing about.
Talking fast
because I'm not quite sure of what I'm saying.
Feeling close kin to the Ugly Duckling.
Not a turkey
yet
not quite a swan.
Pretending I'm "White"
when they tell me I'm "Mexican."
Pretending I'm "Mexican"
when they tell me I'm "White."

"Hey, Boss Man!"
Wherever you are
in Heaven
or in Hell
I'm not fussy.
I just want someone to tell me which line this is
                              I forget

Laughing Last

by Inez Santana

I grew up and live in East Harlem. Some people know it better as El Barrio. It really bothers me when I hear people talking about my culture or where I live because it doesn't make a difference where you are as long as you know what you are going to do in life. Sometimes I dream about making it real good and coming back and showing all the people who have said things about me what I have done in my life.

One day last fall, my sister Gladys and I decided to accompany my sister Letty to 59th Street and Columbus Circle. We got on the number 6 train, just talking about everything that came to our heads. We got off on 42nd Street to take the shuttle. As we were waiting, the train came, but we couldn't get on because something had happened. I think somebody's chain got snatched, or something like that.

Well, the cops opened one of the doors and let out these black and Hispanic teenagers. There were females and males in the group. They all started running or just walking fast. I really didn't pay much attention to this, until I heard these white people speaking to each other and saying all these things about Puerto Ricans, that they are such a disgraceful race and stuff like that. Although I heard what they said, I didn't bother telling my sisters about it.

When they finally let us on the train, we sat down, and some other white guys sat in front of us. This didn't bother us at all—as a matter of fact, we didn't even notice they were there. Until they started speaking. I really didn't hear the details of what they said, but my sisters did. I heard them say a few bad things, but I didn't know they were actually talking about me and my sisters.

My sisters knew that they were talking about us, so they

got really upset. Letty, my older sister, told my other sister, Gladys, to take it calmly, and not to say anything. But I guess the guys took it too far. All of a sudden Letty turned to us and said in a decent manner that she had gone to her friend's house and that she and a few of her friends were having a conversation about people, and she said, "We came to the conclusion that all Hispanics and blacks should come together and kill all the whites that were prejudiced."

I started laughing because the way she said it was so funny. I didn't want to laugh, but I just couldn't hold it back. Gladys has a very loud laugh, so when she started laughing, the guys that were talking stopped. But when we stopped laughing, the guys started talking about us again. This really got me upset. I was about to make a big scene when my sister said, "Don't lower yourself to the level they say you're at." So I just shut my mouth.

Finally our stop came. I felt as if it had taken us forty hours to get there, even though the shuttle only has one stop. I guess they thought all Hispanics were alike. Maybe one day they'll finally learn that we are not all alike and that Hispanics are not all ignorant and that we are getting an education.

When we got off the train we were laughing again at what had just happened, even though we all knew it wasn't something to laugh at.

Corazón

by Djassi Johnson, Luz Otero, Millie Rivera,
Sara Rodríguez, and Simeko Watkins

Corazón was just stepping out of the cab when she
noticed the children playing in front of the tall brown building. As the taxi driver removed her baggage from the trunk,
Corazón asked her mother, Marina, "What are those children doing?"

Marina answered, "They are playing regular games. It's
natural."

"Natural? Oh God, they are so indecent."

"Corazón!" Marina yelled. "Oh never mind—your father
said that it would be difficult. Let's just take your baggage
and go upstairs. Come on, take one."

"What? Isn't there supposed to be a maid to carry the
bags?"

"Oh, no, my child. In New York City you must learn to
live for yourself."

"In that case, I don't like the beginning of this vacation."

"Do you need any help?" asked a young boy.

"Thank you. At least there are some decent people in
this neighborhood."

As they were going up the stairs, Corazón heard a lot of
racket. She heard arguments, babies crying, and saw two
girls playing in the halls. Corazón just stared at them. The
girls were wearing shorts and summer shirts. Corazón was
wearing a fancy dress.

"Mother, are those girls fourteen, like me?" Marina nodded yes. "You mean that girl is fourteen, and she plays with
children in the halls?" She didn't wait for her mother to
answer. She turned around quickly, "Oh here, young boy,
two dollars for being kind enough to carry my bags."

The young boy just stared at her and refused the money

by saying, "It was no problem, thank you anyway."

When Corazón entered the apartment, it smelled delicious. It smelled of homemade food. The lingering odor of fried chicken filled the air. Corazón just stared as she looked at the small apartment. She saw the door of the first room and in there was a bureau and a twin bed. That was all. She followed the aroma of the fried chicken through the apartment. Then she entered another room with a big bed and two bureaus. Corazón asked, "Mother, who will sleep in the first room?"

"You will. Don't worry, it's comfortable, and I will buy you a set of covers with matching curtains," replied her mother.

"Well I expected to have a beautiful bedroom set."

"I don't have the money, so you will have to use what I have supplied for you. I can't give you all that your father gives you."

"Boy, I sure didn't expect any of this." Corazón put her suitcase on the bed, and opened it to unpack. Marina hurried to the kitchen, where she had cooked a nice small dinner for the two of them. She cooked rice and beans with fried chicken. By the time she put everything on the table, Corazón was starving and glad to eat. After they finished eating Marina asked Corazón if she had enjoyed the food.

"Yes mother," Corazón answered. Then she admitted, "In fact, it is better than the food I ate in Daddy's house. More homemade, not frozen food."

The next day Marina took Corazón downstairs to look around the neighborhood and to get acquainted with the people. She told Corazón to put on some cozy shorts and a blouse because it was very warm outside. Instead, Corazón put on her brand new suit. Later they went to the park to look around and to see how the girls acted and also so that Corazón could meet them. A tall, pretty girl approached Corazón. "Hello, my name is Marisela, and yours?"

"My name is Corazón. I came to have a visit with my

mother this summer. I'm fourteen, how old are you?"

"I'm also fourteen. Would you like to play with me?"

"No! I would ruin my new outfit."

"Well we wouldn't want that to happen," answered Marisela sarcastically. "See you later." After Marisela left, Corazón thought to herself, I don't believe that girl is so immature. She plays jump rope with those other girls. They are not sophisticated at all. Or maybe it's that I'm too sophisticated.

Marina watched Marisela and the other girls walk away. Gently, she approached Corazón and asked why she didn't want to play with the girls. Corazón didn't answer. With a question in the sound of her voice, Marina said, "They seemed to be very nice.

"I didn't want to ruin my suit. It's brand new. Daddy bought it for me." Corazón was pouting.

"It's very beautiful," Marina said with exasperation, "and I bet it cost him a lot too, but I'm sure you don't have to worry about getting it dirty."

"Daddy would kill me."

"You mean to tell me your father gets mad because you get dirty?"

"Well usually María, our maid, cleans it up before he sees it."

Marina stared at her. "I think you depend too much on other people." Corazón felt hurt, but Marina took her hand, and they began to walk. Corazón looked at her mother as they crossed the street, and finally got the nerve to ask her the question that had been bothering her, "What really happened between you and daddy? I want to know your side of the story."

"It's a long story, but I guess we have the time. I met your father when we were seventeen. Well, it may sound silly, but it's true what they say about love at first sight. But we weren't too happy because we had a lot of pressure from our family. So we decided to elope together."

"And you made it fine with just the two of you. No money or support from your families."

"Yes, we both got jobs, though it was hard, and afterwards our families began to understand why we eloped."

"When did I come along?"

"You came later, and we were so happy. And our parents were also happy about being grandparents. Everything was going so well afterwards. We even thought your father was getting a promotion. But he didn't get it. He heard it around the job that he didn't get it because he was married to a Hispanic woman. Well, I couldn't hold him back. At first he didn't want to face that it was me who was causing the problems, but then one night he came home drunk, screaming, 'I want a divorce.' The next day he took action, hiring a lawyer and all. He also won the battle for custody. Now he started to remember that I missed you, so he sent you here for the summer so we could get to know each other."

"That's pretty much what daddy told me." Corazón felt sad, though she couldn't put her sadness into words. Marina felt sorry for her and tried to think of a way to cheer her up. She suggested they go shopping together. Corazón loved the idea. They went home to get Marina's pocketbook and a few other things. While they were there, the phone rang. "I got it," said her mother. Marina was in the middle of a good conversation with her friend Concha when she heard Corazón yell, "Mother, Mother, hurry please come!"

Marina put down the phone and ran, yelling across the apartment, "What is it Corazón?"

"There's a roach on the wall!"

"Corazón there's nothing to be afraid of, it cannot hurt you," Marina said under the breath of a giggle.

"But mother, it's gross," Corazón said in a pleading voice.

"Well you better get used to it—you are going to see lots more."

194

"But mo . . ."

"Look, Corazón, I'll try my best to keep them away, but for now you are going to have to get used to it."

"Yes mother," Corazón said reluctantly. Marina, now satisfied, told Corazón to straighten things up in the kitchen but then suddenly remembered her phone call. She picked up the receiver and told her friend Concha, "It was nothing, my daughter saw a roach."

There was silence on the other line; then Concha asked, "So how are you enjoying your daughter's visit?"

Replying breathlessly, Marina answered, "Concha, I'm enjoying it a lot. At times she can be a brat, but I love her so much! I don't want her to go." Her conversation was interrupted when Corazón called from the other room, "Ready!" Marina hung up the phone, and told Corazón that they would meet Concha and her daughter Rosie at the store. Marina knew how many things Corazón's father was always buying her; deep in her heart she was jealous and hoped to win some of Corazón's love by buying her presents.

When they got to the store, there were so many beautiful things that Corazón wanted. Marina showed Corazón some very nice clothing that was quite popular around El Barrio. But Corazón didn't like these clothes; she preferred the type of clothes that were popular in her predominantly white school.

"But Corazón, those clothes are too expensive here, and I don't think they're worth so much money," said Marina. She held up the clothes that she had picked out and said, "Try these—they look nicer and almost all the girls around the block are wearing them. And plus you can get more of them since they're not so expensive."

"But mother, they're ugly and they're not my style. Anyway money's no object, Daddy's going to send me money weekly. Plus I have some money on me that he gave me until I get my first allowance."

Marina sighed. Corazón's father was still getting all of

the credit even when he was miles away. At that moment Rosie and Concha approached them at the cashier. Corazón saw Rosie with all the clothes that her mother had earlier showed her. Then Rosie asked, "Why don't you buy clothes like these?"

"Oh, I just don't like those type of clothes and only those Puerto Ric . . ." At that moment she noticed that she had let out that she still could not admit that she was Puerto Rican. She felt uncomfortable next to them and couldn't get accustomed to their way of living.

Rosie was shocked and all she could say was, Oh. Rosie lowered her head in shame and embarrassment. Corazón felt very bad. "I really didn't mean it the way it came out."

The mothers didn't hear a thing of the girls' conversation. They were talking while Concha's mother paid the cashier, and the four of them left the store. As they walked, two boys came up to Rosie and said hello. Concha turned and said with a wink, "You see, Corazón, Rosie has so many friends, and maybe she'll introduce you to one."

Rosie introduced Corazón to Miguel and his friend Davy. Rosie went out with Davy behind her mother's back. Davy gave her a hello kiss. Miguel just stood there staring at Corazón. "This is Marina's daughter?" asked Davy. He was surprised for Corazón didn't look anything like her mother. Corazón had blond hair, and Marina was a brunette. "Corazón is a very nice name," he said.

"Yeah. You just stole my Corazón away with your beauty and charm," said Miguel.

"Thank you. You're very kind."

Afterwards the girls went home with their mothers and Corazón and Rosie started talking about what had happened earlier. "I really am sorry. I didn't mean it, it just slipped out," Corazón apologized.

"It's OK. I didn't think you meant it. It's just that you're so used to living with your father and that neighborhood . . .

196

PREJUDICE

it came out without your noticing really what you said. When two people become friends, it's hard to break them up."

Rosie may have forgiven her but Corazón knew they would never be as close as they would have been if she hadn't made the earlier comment. But she still hoped they could be friends. Then they started talking about the guys they were in love with. Corazón confided to Rosie that she liked Miguel, but she didn't know whether he was the type to rush into things or what.

"Miguel isn't that bad, but I went out with him once, and after two months he dumped me."

"You say it so proudly. Aren't you just a bit sad?"

"No. And anyway I have Davy. You don't have to worry though because you'll be gone in less than two months."

The next day the girls were outside together when they heard Miguel's voice from behind. "Hi there, beautiful." Corazón was a bit surprised. Thinking about what he had done to her friend, she felt uneasy near him. He tried to kiss her, and she moved away.

"I'm sorry, but I just don't want to be like that with you. Just friends. O.K.?"

"What do you mean? I was just going to give you a hello kiss on the cheek. Or did you expect something different from me? I wasn't even thinking of kissing you like that. You're white, and like the rest of your people, you take everything too serious."

"You mean to tell me that you weren't going to try anything funny? You didn't think of me in that way?"

"No. Just because you come from a high class neighborhood and down here in El Barrio you think you're better than anybody else . . . well you're not. Just like when you told Rosie that the clothes she wears are Puerto Rican clothes. Are you prejudiced? If you're going to stay here, I think you should really get used to the way we live here."

Corazón felt very bad. She had known all along that she

was not going to get used to the way these Puerto Ricans lived. In fact, she noticed that she kept saying "these" Puerto Ricans. She realized that she was prejudiced in a way. Prejudiced against her own people. She was half-Puerto Rican, and she didn't know a thing about them.

Corazón ran home to her mother. She was humiliated and embarrassed. Even Rosie, the girl she thought was her friend, would never be really close to her. She told her mother the whole story, and her mother sympathized with her. Corazón wanted to go home. She wanted to be with her father.

The next morning a cab came out front to pick her up. She was ready to leave. She wasn't going to stay another day and could hardly wait to kiss her mother good-bye and get into the cab. "Good-bye Corazón," called Marina.

Marina knew that she probably would never see her daughter again, that Corazón would never understand this side of her life; she could not see how she could have two different cultures. Instead she chose to limit herself to just one. Marina could not do a thing but feel sorry for her.

INCOGNITO

by Denise Alcalá

You stare blankly
at me—
bare-faced,
with naked eyes
and repeat
that I
have not
been punished
for being
female
Chicana
or short

ah, it's
so easy to
be naive
when you
are born
with pale
skin and green dancing
eyes

you were so
resentful
that day they
aimed their
"honky hate" at you
and relating
it to me
angered you more
for I could

only lend you
a soft, low
chuckle
that I had
carefully rehearsed
over the years

CHAPTER 9

MAKING IT

Interview with Ingrid Ramos: A Friend of East Harlem

by Shanique García, Ileana Morales, Malika Mosley, Enike Smith with Laura González, Stephanie Metzger, Leslie Rivera, and Nereida Román

The excitement began as we walked from 99th to 109th Street for our first interview of the year. Although it was a cold November afternoon, the distance from our school to P.S. 83, where we were to meet Ingrid Ramos, seemed only a short distance. Ingrid Ramos had been a special teacher of Ileana Morales, one of our "mujeres," eight years ago when Ileana was in kindergarten. She helped Ileana with her reading because, at that time, Ileana spoke only Spanish. We chose to interview Ms. Ramos because she had influenced and inspired Ileana during her younger years.

We entered the four-story building and waited nervously while Ileana went to find Ms. Ramos. We stared down P.S. 83's long, glossy hallway—the hall looked as if it would never end—and then we saw an image. It was Ingrid Ramos. She was short and had a tan complexion. Her hair was black and a little past her shoulders in length. She wore a nice gray business suit and walked with confidence.

Ms. Ramos greeted us with a sweet and warm hello and then led us into a small, compact room that seemed to be a classroom. We sat down on old, squeaky wooden chairs and assembled ourselves in a circle around her. Quietly, we looked around the room: we were not sure how to begin our interview. It seemed that she didn't mind the wait as she got comfortable herself. After the first few questions we, as a team, began to feel more confident.

Ms. Ramos answered our questions with ease and an occasional laugh. The way she spoke made us also feel at ease; she treated us as real interviewers who had a job to get done and not as kids. She answered us with long detailed answers that left us speechless. Each word held our interest. She spoke like someone who didn't have a care in the world.

Ms. Ramos has been teaching in District 4 in Harlem for twenty-one years and has enjoyed every moment of it. She thinks the people in Harlem have a lot to offer and wants everyone to know that. She taught at P.S. 112 first and has been at P.S. 83 since 1980. She has held positions ranging from director to aerobics teacher (for kids in kindergarten and first grade). But she especially loves working with children from kindergarten to second grade. "I love to teach," she said.

Eight years ago she tried the job of director because she wanted a change, but she didn't like it so much and missed the classroom, so she went back to doing what she loves the most, teaching. "I love to work directly with children," she said to explain her short time as director. "I love children, and I always wanted to be a teacher," she said, which was amazing, because we, as children, have changed our career ideas for the future many times. Her job now is assistant director at B.B.M.S., Bilingual Bicultural Mini School.

"I was born in New York," she said, "but my parents are from Puerto Rico." She went to Puerto Rico with her parents when she was two but moved back in time to attend second grade. When she came back to New York, she and her family moved into the projects on 99th Street and Madison Avenue, and she lived there until college. She remembers living on the 15th floor during the big blackout of the early 1960s when the elevators weren't working. For a kid, it was fun.

Ingrid Ramos is a city person; she loves the variety of people and activities that city life can offer. Her parents had been the supers of a tenement building, and the projects were a big step for them. We followed up on that by asking her if the projects were better back then. "It wasn't until the late sixties that the projects began to change," she said.

204

MAKING IT

First there were gangs, and now drugs have taken over.

Ms. Ramos thinks family life is very valuable. She is the second oldest of five children. She has one older brother, two younger brothers and one younger sister. Her family was not rich, and her parents were very strict, but she has fond memories of her childhood. She remembers rides through Central Park, and that Central Park was their all-time playground. "I had a fun childhood . . . we did everything together." To her, family is important. Though she also liked being with her friends, she was never allowed to hang out, and she wasn't allowed to spend the night at other people's houses until she was in high school.

Ms. Ramos' parents wanted their children to have a good education. Her mother had been a teacher in Puerto Rico. She told us how a lot of times she wasn't allowed to go outside, so she and her siblings developed a love for board games. And as a young girl, she loved to read, and she still does.

Ms. Ramos said the lowest point in her life was when her father died when she was thirteen years old. Her mother is sixty-eight years old now. Her family still is very close, and Ms. Ramos seems very proud of that. She and her family still try to get together whenever they can. In fact, she spends most of the holidays with her family.

Ms. Ramos attended Marymount Manhattan College where she majored in Spanish. She was one of the only two Puerto Ricans in the school, but she never had any problems because she was Hispanic. Though she has never really suffered from prejudice, she feels that too many people expect people of different races to act in certain ways. Ms. Ramos now lives in Sheepshead Bay, Brooklyn, and when she moved, it was the first time she really had any problems with prejudice. She thinks that people are not born prejudiced but are taught.

She discussed other issues with us. For example, peer pressure. She thinks that girls have more pressure put on them sexually, and suffer more from the consequences, but both boys and girls have pressures. Boys have the pressure of proving themselves as men—the macho pressure. But for both boys and girls, she told us, "I think that you can love and be loved without demonstrating it by sex." When she was faced with the question, "What do you think of abortion?" she replied that whether or not a girl chose to have an abortion was the girl's decision. She told us teen pregnancy has nothing to do with race, that it happens with all races, but some people are able to hide it more than others.

The next few questions we asked her were on political parties and issues. She thinks voting is important and that Hispanics should be more political and take a stand on issues. "I've grown to feel I can make a difference," Ms. Ramos told us. The next question we asked was if she thought equal rights existed. "Equal rights don't really exist," she said, "and equal rights will never exist, but we can't make that an excuse for not accomplishing what we want." We have a long way to go.

Ms. Ramos was never married, and she never had children. That was a surprise to hear because she likes children so much. She lives with her mother and feels her life is satisfying and busy the way it is now. The children she teaches have become like her own children, and she wants to be a role model for them, the way she was for Ileana Morales. As she explained to us, "When you see more role models, you begin to think, 'I can do it too.'"

Besides her work with children in the schools, Ms. Ramos is also active at church and has worked with the homeless and the elderly. She said, "I love working with people. I'm a people person!" She dreams of being rich someday and using her money to help out the community and the homeless.

Another thing Ms. Ramos loves to do is travel. She's been to Europe a couple of times and would like to go again. She has also driven across the United States and back four or five times. There are some places she hasn't been that she would like to visit—for example, Hawaii, Alaska, and Australia.

We asked her a lot of questions about death. She answered all of them. For example, we asked her if she died, how she would want everyone to remember her. She said she would like people to remember her as a sweet, loving, caring person who always gave her all and always looked for the best in people. That's how we'll always remember her.

At the close of our interview she said, "If you have a goal that you want to achieve, then you should try your best to do so." She also said, "Always see yourself as a person who has something to offer."

We thanked Ingrid Ramos for her time and her wonderful answers. We will always remember the day we interviewed her. She gave us a feeling of joy.

Interview with Olga Méndez: The Senator from El Barrio

by Shanique García, Laura González, Ileana Morales,
Malika Mosley, and Enike Smith

We left school at about two o'clock in the afternoon and took the bus uptown to 116th Street and First Avenue. Senator Méndez's office was only two blocks away, on Third Avenue, but we took the crosstown bus anyway—it was an extremely cold day.

Her office was above a small department store. In order to get in, we had to ring a bell and walk up one flight of very steep stairs to an unlocked door. Behind the door was a secretary and several other people behind desks. It was a dull smoke-filled room, and we had to wait a short while. We sat patiently as the workers communicated among themselves in Spanish. We were surrounded by posters of Olga, brochures, desks, and people.

When she walked in, we all sat quite shocked for we didn't recognize her. She greeted us in Spanish and led us into her small office. Hanging on the walls were nineteen different plaques and awards for what Olga had done in the past years to help her community and other causes. There were no windows in her office and it was sort of warm, so we had to turn on the air conditioner, even though it was a cold winter day.

We formed a semi circle around her desk as she lit her first of many Kent cigarettes. She let out a puff and, with a thick Spanish accent, asked each one of us our names and where we came from. Then she told us about herself. She told us she was proud and comfortable to have been born in Puerto Rico. She was proud to have parents of Puerto Rican heritage. Olga told us that when she was nine years old, her mother passed away. Her father became a very big influence on her. Although her father had to raise Olga, her five sisters and one brother, he made it his business to make sure his kids had an education. Education was very important in her family, and her father believed that was true for his daughters as well as his son.

In 1956 after graduating from the University of Puerto Rico, Olga decided to come to N.Y. She attended Columbia University and received a Master's degree. She married but is now a widow and has no children.

Olga loves East Harlem. She says that most of the people are decent human beings, and she doesn't like it when people put down the area. The drug problem is a problem all over the U.S., not just East Harlem. She thinks that if a parent has a son or daughter who is a drug addict, you have to decide either to sacrifice yourself or kick out your kid and tell him or her to go and get help. Also, if a child is selling drugs, a parent doesn't want the younger children to be affected.

We asked Olga why she didn't like to use the term "Hispanic." She leaned back in her chair and answered, "Well you see, I don't like the term Hispanic because it's too broad, it's too general. Being called Hispanic is not being clearly identified, and all definitions are political in nature." Instead, she felt that people should know their roots, and have pride in their own background, whether Puerto Rican, Dominican, Mexican, Cuban, Colombian—whatever country. She feels sorry for people who don't know their past.

Some Americans feel that Puerto Ricans are not citizens of the United States because we have a different language and culture. Many people are ignorant about the history of Puerto Rico, including ourselves, even though there are so many Puerto Ricans in our schools. For example, we didn't know about Mrs. González from Isabella, Puerto Rico who won the first federal civil rights case for Puerto Ricans when she fought for the right to travel freely through the United States.

The 1980 Census showed that Hispanics were the most numerous minority in this country. Why are we called a minority, then, if there are so many of us? Senator Méndez fears a reaction against Hispanics now, and she used as an example the government's securing the borders to block Hispanics from coming into the country. Are people scared Hispanics are going to change everything and take over?

When asked the question, "Why does it seem that minority girls get pregnant at an earlier age than 'white girls'?" she replied, "It is only a myth. Most white people have the money for an abortion, whereas most minorities don't." The statistics on abortions for white and wealthy women are not so clear. She seemed disturbed by the question because her voice sounded upset as she told us, "I do not accept at all that minority teenagers get pregnant more often than white teenagers." But she also told us that overall "whites are the poorest in the nation" and used Appalachia as an example.

Olga spoke intelligently about many subjects. She was enthusiastic and self-confident. She had a strong idea of the way things should be, and was very opinionated. She told us "the poor have to energize themselves" to get funds and programs that they can benefit from.

We knew that Hispanics have been called "The Sleeping Giant" because we do not have enough political power. But Olga is the kind of person who can show us how to make breaks with the past. She herself did it when she became the first Puerto Rican woman elected to office on the mainland and, in 1978, the first woman state senator.

In the last presidential election, 1988, Olga supported Michael Dukakis and believed in his policies. She was sad when he lost, as were most of us. She liked his plan in Massachusetts to use tax money so that women on public assistance could go to school and training projects so they could get good jobs. He ran a successful program and the women could earn more money than if they stayed on public assistance. In the end, they cost the state less money.

Impressed with our group, Olga encouraged us to also break with the past. She said, "Being a woman, you can do anything anyone else in the world does." She also added, "Ideas do not have a sex." With self-discipline and hard work, we too can achieve. At the end of our interview, Olga reminded us to always "treasure and protect" our own personhood.

Interview with Nicholasa Mohr: Hold Fast to Your Dreams

By Kim Baez, Michelle Calero, Luz Otero,
Monique Rubio, and Janel Shepard

When Nicholasa Mohr, the author of *Nilda*, came to our school, the young women in our class prepared a feast of Spanish food to welcome her. We couldn't believe it was Nicholasa herself when she arrived. She looked young and pretty.

We had plenty of food for this special occasion: plátanos, yellow rice, the famous fried chicken made by Kim Baez's mother, lasagna, chocolate cake, tembleque, and cookies. Nicholasa signed her autograph in our copies of *Nilda* and talked to us about her books and her career as a writer. While we feasted, we asked her many questions about whether her book was fiction or non-fiction and whether it was really that hard growing up in Spanish Harlem during the 1940s.

Nicholasa explained that she began as a writer when someone she knew asked her to write a book about her life as a Puerto Rican. She wrote some fifty pages, but her work was rejected. The publisher felt that her writing was not "authentic" enough. He expected stories about drugs and gangs. This is what you would call the typical stereotype of Puerto Ricans. Nicholasa had to go out and find another publisher on her own. Eventually, when Harper & Row gave her a job to design a book jacket, she showed them her stories and they agreed to publish her first book.

Nicholasa told us that most of her books deal mainly with human behavior. She said that she is fascinated with the way people thrive and survive. When she wrote *Nilda*, she took her own memories and then added her imagination to them. Writing the book was a way of sharing her life. But we were surprised that so much of the book was fiction. For example, in order to write *Nilda*, she had to go to the library and do research on the period in the 40s during World War II, a time just before she was born.

All of us thought the book was nonfiction because Nicholasa made the events in the book seem as if they were true. Some events were true for Nicholasa. Her family did break up, she had four brothers, like Nilda, and she was told many times that she was not "really Spanish."

We discovered that Nicholasa was born in El Barrio, where our school is located and where some of us live. Both her parents' families came from Ponce, Puerto Rico. We also found out that she attended P. S. 72. Since she was a little girl, Nicholasa loved to read. She said she "ate" books, and she always had a facility for writing. When you read *Nilda*, you get a peek at this author's young life.

After finishing school, Nicholasa married (twice) and had two sons, both of whom are now grown with lives of their own.

Aside from her books, another subject we spoke about were career choices for Hispanic women. Nicholasa talked about the "old fashioned" ways and how some people still believe that girls have to do the laundry, the cooking, the cleaning, and should stay home and serve their men. The girls in our class are against this, but we still have to live with grandparents, aunts, and uncles who believe in this jibberish.

Nicholasa feels strongly about the need for girls to have careers before they get married. She feels that you should always have some way to support yourself and to feel you can make something of your own life. Like her own mother, she believes you should not give your dreams away.

We believe Nicholasa is a wise woman.

Interview with Tina Ramírez: Founder of Ballet Hispánico

by Ivy Colomba, Millie Rivera, Sara Rodríguez, Monique Rubio, Janel Shepard, Simeko Watkins, and Guadalupe Zárate

Our group went to visit Tina Ramírez, founder and artistic director of Ballet Hispánico. Ballet Hispánico is located on West 89th Street, between Amsterdam and Columbus Avenues. Monique Rubio, one of "las mujeres" attends Ballet Hispánico's dance school, and Ivy Colomba, another "mujer," used to take classes there.

When we went inside, a woman in the office named Josephine called Tina to tell her we had arrived, and then we sat down on chairs in the long hallway. After two minutes Tina arrived. We all greeted her and then followed her into one of the studios. In the studio we nestled comfortably on the floor while Tina spoke to us. She is a beautiful woman who looks as if her whole life has revolved around dancing. She is middle-aged, but has good posture and the body of a dancer. To us, she looked much younger than she actually is.

Tina Ramírez was born into an artistic family in Caracas, Venezuela. She was brought to the United States when she was six years old. Her father had made his career as a bullfighter, and her mother "was destined to be an actress" but never fulfilled her dreams of doing so.

Ever since Tina was very young, she wanted to be a dancer and to perform. Her parents were always supportive, and by the age of thirteen or fourteen, Tina began to fulfill her dreams.

Tina's first interest was ballet. She was inspired by the

work of La Argentinita, and later joined Rhythms of Spain, the same company as La Argentinita's partner. She also danced with the John Butler Company and was on television a number of times. Tina reminded us that "there is no such thing as small parts for true dancers."

Besides dancing and studying dance, Tina was also involved in teaching dance by the time she was seventeen. As soon as she started to teach, she loved it with a passion. She did not do it just for the money. She did it because she wanted to help others learn all about dance. She thought it was a positive force. In April of 1963 the director of the school where Tina was teaching decided to retire and asked Tina to take over.

Tina enjoyed her job very much, but she saw that many of the kids, despite their determination, would not be accepted by dance companies. She wanted to do something for them and was helped by a summer grant that she received during President Johnson's War on Poverty. She used the money to hire the best teachers she could find in New York, including her own teacher, M. R. Corvino. Her students were mostly seven, eight, and nine years old, the best years for beginning to study dance, according to Tina. They were able to attend without charge, but the funding was later cut.

This did not hold Tina back. Her past success helped her to go on to form her own new company, Ballet Hispánico. This time she received funding from New York State's Council of the Arts when Rockefeller was governor. Tina's company began with six girls and two boys ranging in age from twelve to fourteen. They prepared to do "street theater" in the summer. For six weeks they performed five or six times a week in Brooklyn, Manhattan, and the Bronx using a truck with a platform that opened up to twenty feet by twenty feet. The dancers shared a small dressing room that fit into a corner of the stage. They had great team work and togetherness. More and more people started joining the company, and it became a tremendous success.

Ballet Hispánico is now seventeen years old. Tina and her company travel throughout the United States and around the world. During this summer, Ballet Hispánico will be going to Italy and Spain. Just hearing about these things makes us feel great because we see that it never hurts to dream.

Tina explained to us why she named the company Ballet Hispánico. She said "ballet" stands for any type of dancing that has a story and "Hispánico" stands for the twenty-three countries where Spanish is spoken. As Tina told us, in this hemisphere, Hispanics are not a minority—we are a majority.

When we asked Tina what some of the obstacles to her success were, she said that her main and only obstacle was that her mind and thoughts were way ahead of her time. She was trying to get Hispanics to become more interested in art and theater, and they were thinking more about their clothing and, because their wages were so low, their housing and food.

Spanish women: Tina feels that often they are usually at home, cooking, cleaning, and caring for children. She said that to her, learning how to read is more important than anything else. As she pointed out, if you know how to read, all you have to do is get a cookbook to learn how to cook!

Tina Ramírez never did get married. Her career always came first, and she thought she could always get married later on. For all women, she feels it is stupid to marry just to be supported. She said one of the most important things for all teenage girls to learn is how to make their own living. And then to be the best you can at something. No matter what that something may be, you should feel proud of what you can do. Be an individual. What other people think of you should not matter: "You were born alone and you will die alone." She urged us not to be lazy and to learn a profession so that any place in the world we might find ourselves, we would be able to support ourselves.

Tina Ramírez has contributed much to our society and many ought to appreciate her accomplishments. By learning about her life, we see how thinking positive equals zero obstacles and mucho success. That goes to show what you can do if you really want something.

Bibliography

Alcalá, Denise. "Abuela," *Revista Chicano-Riqueña*, 1978.
—"incognito," *Revista Chicano-Riqueña*, 1978.

Ali, Amina Susan. "Memories of Her," *Cuentos: Stories by Latinas*,
    Kitchen Table: Women of Color Press, 1983.
—"Teenage Zombie," *Cuentos: Stories by Latinas*, Kitchen Table:
    Women of Color Press, 1983.

Arenas, Rosa María. "Dream in the Hospital," *The Americas Review*,
    1990.
—"La Rosa Mordida," *The Americas Review*, 1990.

Cervantes, Lorna Dee. "Refugee Ship," *Revista Chicano-Riqueña*, 1975.
—"The Beauty of Me and My People," *Revista Chicano-Riqueña*, 1981.
—"Thinking," *Revista Chicano-Riqueña*, 1981.
—"This Morning There Were Rainbows in the Sprinklers," *Kikirikí*,
    Arte Público Press, 1990.
—"Which Line Is This? I Forget," *Revista Chicano-Riqueña*, 1981.

Cofer, Judith Ortiz. "El Olvido," *The Americas Review*, 1986.
    "First Love," *Silent Dancing*, Arte Público Press, 1990.
—"Fulana," *The Americas Review*, 1988.
—"Lost Relatives," *Terms of Survival*, Arte Público Press, 1987.
—"Mamacita," *Terms of Survival*, Arte Público Press, 1987.
—"María Sabida," *Silent Dancing*, Arte Público Press, 1990.
—"Origen," *The Americas Review*, 1986.
—"So Much for Mañana," *The Americas Review*, 1986.
—"They Say," *Silent Dancing*, Arte Público Press, 1990.
—"Vida," *Silent Dancing*, Arte Público Press, 1990.

Engle, Margarita Mondrus. "Niña," *The Americas Review*, 1987.

Fernández, Roberta. "Amanda," *Intaglio*, Arte Público Press, 1990.

González, Cristina. "To a Woman I Love," *Revista Chicano-Riqueña*,
    1983.

Hospital, Caroline. "Bedtime story," *The Americas Review*, 1989.
—"Dear Tía," *The Americas Review*, 1989.

Llano, María Elena. "In the Family," *Short Stories by Latin American
    Women, The Magic and the Real*, Arte Público Press, 1990.

Mendell, Olga. "Listening to Mongo Santamaría Calling the Spirits
    from Buffalo," *The Americas Review*, 1986.

Mohr, Nicholasa. "Christmas Was a Time of Plenty," *Revista Chicano-Riqueña*, 1980.

—"Esperanza," *Nilda*, Arte Público Press, 1986.

—"A Very Special Pet," *El Bronx Remembered*. Arte Público Press, 1986.

Mora, Pat. "Elena," *Woman of Her Word*, Arte Público Press, 1983.

Muñoz, Amina. "María," *Revista Chicano-Riqueña*, 1980.

Piñón, Evangelina Vigil. "remolino en mi taza," *Thirty an' Seen a Lot*, Arte Público Press, 1985.

—"mento joven: nothin' like a pensive child," *Thirty an' Seen a Lot*, Arte Público Press, 1985.

Pursifull, Carmen M. "The Poltergeist," *The Americas Review*, 1983.

Yzquierdo, Rosa Elena. "Six Take Away One," *The Americas Review*, 1986.

—"Abuela," *The Americas Review*, 1986.

Zambosco, Elsa. "A Vanessa," *Revista Chicano-Riqueña*, 1981.

Baez, Kim. "Interview with Nicholasa Mohr: Hold Fast to Your Dreams."

Calero, Michelle. "I Thought You Loved Me."

—"Interview with Nicholasa Mohr: Hold Fast to Your Dreams."

Colomba, Ivy. "A Lost Friend."

—"Interview with Tina Ramírez: Founder of Ballet Hispánico."

García, Shanique. "Braces and Intelligence."

—"Interview with Ingrid Ramos: A Friend of East Harlem."

González, Laura. "Interview with Ingrid Ramos: A Friend of East Harlem."

—"Interview with Olga Méndez: The Senator from El Barrio."

Johnson, Djassi. "Corazón."

Martin, Carmen. "Do It To the Music."

Metzger, Stephanie. "Interview with Ingrid Ramos: A Friend of East Harlem."

Shepard, Janel. "Interview with Nicholasa Mohr: Hold Fast to Your Dreams."

—"Interview with Tina Ramírez: Founder of Ballet Hispánico."

Smith, Enike. "A Man So Special."

—"Interview with Ingrid Ramos: A Friend of East Harlem."

—"Interview with Olga Méndez: The Senator from El Barrio."

Tiburcio, Jeanette. "Anita Lake Rojas."

Watkins, Simeko. "Corazón."

—"Interview with Tina Ramírez: Founder of Ballet Hispánico."

Zárate, Guadalupe. "Interview with Tina Ramírez: Founder of Ballet Hispánico."